Contemporary Accents in Liberal Religion

1960

Selected by Bradford E. Gale

Beacon Press Beacon Hill Boston

Acknowledgments

The editor wishes to thank the following publications for permission to reprint the articles under their control:

Congress Weekly, A Review of Jewish Interests, for "Between Man and Man" by Jack Mendelsohn, November 18, 1957;

Phylon, The Atlanta University Review of Race and Culture, for "The Changing South: Revolution or Reconciliation" by Edward A. Cahill, July 1958.

Table of Contents

iii

The Commitment: *Practical Religion*

Prefatory Note

This volume of contemporary literary expression in the field of liberal religion has been gathered in the conviction that man is inspired today as much as he has ever been — that "among the living of these days there is as much of the Holy Spirit as ever breathed in any age."[1] Most of the selections are from ministers and laymen who are avowed Unitarians and Universalists, but some show affinity to our thought by writers in other communions.

Whatever it is in man that inspires him touches him first of all through the direct, elemental experiences of life. Poetry comes nearest of all literary forms to preserving the immediacy of these experiences. All true religion finds its expression first of all in poetry. So the contemporary accents in this volume are first expressed through poems.

Man also attempts to define and interpret these primary, sensitive contacts with reality. He calls these attempts "theology." The second portion of this volume presents some definitive articles which express the intellectual content, the reflective second thought, of contemporary religious liberalism.

The final section comprises representative articles on the social significance of religion and on contemporary social concerns. As they seek to excite thought and feeling into action, they validate in human terms the religious venture.

Vital religion begins in the individual as he learns to keep his emotional health while confronting the most painful of life's experiences and as he gathers understanding from them. It grows as he learns to express and communicate this understanding. It reaches its peak in his courageous commitment to advance the kind of individual and social welfare which fosters in every man the freedom to express the meaning of life in his own way.

---

(1) Robert L. Cope, ed., *Indictments and Invitations*, Boston, Council of Liberal Churches, 1959, p. 3.

This volume of *Accents* attempts to show in a limited way that contemporary religious liberalism in America has all the aspects of a vital religion — as evinced in its creative poetry, its realistic theology and its prophetic utterance.

Bradford E. Gale

UNITED FIRST PARISH CHURCH
QUINCY, MASSACHUSETTS
JANUARY 1960

The Experience

Poetry

From the whispering frontiers of life, religion talks of
infinites.

BORIS PASTERNAK

Notes on Contributors

Karl M. Chworowsky is minister emeritus of the First Unitarian Church of Fairfield County in Westport, Connecticut.

Arthur Graham is minister of the Oak Ridge Unitarian Church in Oak Ridge, Tennessee.

Hazel Rogers Gredler is minister emeritus of two churches in Massachusetts, the Unitarian Congregational Society of Barnstable and the First Universalist-Unitarian Church of Yarmouth.

Vlyn Johnson, deceased, was a member of The First Congregational Society in Salem, Massachusetts.

Ford Lewis is associate minister of the First Unitarian Church in Portland, Oregon.

John G. MacKinnon is minister of the All Souls Unitarian Church in Indianapolis, Indiana.

Roscoe E. Trueblood is minister of the First Parish in Cohasset, Massachusetts.

Jennifer Leigh

July 4, 1956-July 4, 1956

Laid in a quiet corner of the world,
I was so little, and you knew me not.
Yet here in this lovely place, I see the moon
And feel the sun's warm rays.   The many-fingered
Rain finds me, and I feel the movement of
Life's growing things. You must not grieve for me.
Death does not change our love for one another:
That love will still live on; it does not lessen,
Always I am yours, and you are mine.
Sometimes the heart asks more than life can give,
But Peace will come, and it will make us wise.

Hazel Rogers Gredler

Easter

I feel the breath of Spring far off, far off.
The grass takes on the hue of green, while birds
And leaves and broken ground give forth the scent
Of fragrant April-time, and swallows weave
In flight across the sky with shimmering sound.
My feet stray toward the shore, and there, amid
The beating sea and crested foam of waves,
I stand. As far as eye can see, rolls on
The blue of sky and surge that meet the smooth
And tawny beach — and out again, where cloud
And water verge. The wind blows rampant with
The wine of speed. In ecstasy I lift
My outstretched arms — this, Our Eternity —
O God, I pray, help me to carry far
This message to the world: that though we seem
To writhe in bitterness and waste of life,
Yet these shall pass away. The eternal dawn
Of Life and Beauty from the soul of earth
Transcends all pain and grief. The years will come
And go, but always ever there — the sea,
The stars so unconcerned, the apple blooms,
The warm, dark ground from which shall spring new life.
The faithful beauty of the world goes on!

Hazel Rogers Gredler

The Great Nonconformist

Black man, red man, yellow man and white —
All the shades and tones between, mingling dark and light:
All of human substance in the Maker's sight.

How else could that Artist give this world its color?
Only dull men still prefer duplicate and dollar,
Seeing sameness safer and thereby growing duller.

White man, black man, yellow man and red —
All of human substance, when all's done and said,
Yet He makes not two alike, else all art were dead.

Vlyn Johnson

Credo

If God exists, and I believe He must,
Shall I not find Him in the silence white
Of time-worn stars a-tremble through the night
And in the lowly things of earth and dust?

If God exists — and dare I say Him nay?
Will He not speak through every common hour
A syllable of beauty and of power
And fill with haunting echoes every day?

If God exists — Help Thou my unbelief!
I too shall find Him where a brother's face,
Lust-scarred and dull, reveals a finer grace.
Did He not speak His promise to a thief?

If God exists — O blessed faith and true,
I've found Him in the radiant soul of You!

Karl M. Chworowsky

The Types of the Spirit

There are all classes and conditions of spirit.
Some move through the garrets of life
Fingering patterns on the dry dust of ancient furniture.
Others can live only in fine rooms
Where glass panes deflect the white and the wet alike
And reflect sun and all beauty only through angles of the glass.
There are those who march in unison to the drum beat,
Obedient to echeloned command to die irresponsibly.
Fearful of the day and their own need for identity,
The craven ones populate only the night and its shadows.
For such as these there is neither God nor Humanity,
And their spirit knows not duration nor intensity.
It is pulverous and hard, in constant erosion into nothingness.

Blessed, therefore, is the spirit that strides the paths of life with
    joy,
Forward looking, daring the day, challenging the night,
Seeking promise, not plan; hopeful, faithful, secure;
Whose laughter, echoing down the valleys of time,
Confirms that to walk erect is prelude to the flight of aspiration.
To such as these the earth-bound man looks up and says:
"That man is free. He dares the journey."
So may we.

Arthur Graham

The Fortress Mind

The mind can be a fortress,
Thick-walled and invulnerable,
Close-formed in the sprawling
Plain of life; an armed island
Of isolation against the emptiness,
Where only assumed enemies move;
Open only to the lonely sky.
Such a mind is also a prison
Incarcerating the memories of yesterday
In brightness worked by the constant
Polish of desire, and where
The outer world viewed from the ramparts
Is ever a hated desert, however green.
Such a fortress can only die
Before howl of wind or sear of sun;
For even as it fingers against a barren sky
The targets of its booming death,
It curls, erodes and dies — a static thing
To which even nature is opposed.
She clears, if slowly, the neutral earth,
So man may move and probe and know
And see the flowers beneath his feet
When he escapes his self-made tomb
And goes forth to life.

This thing, once seen in all the earth,
Must come to pass in us.
It is wisdom to topple such walls
And be free upon the land.

Arthur Graham

8

The Past and Present

Ancient cathedrals on sleepy slopes
Rise like the wraiths of ancient monks
To stir in the heart the half-forgotten cadence
Of marches with old crusaders
In the panoply of religious wars.
What was then real is now but art.
The achievements of man's seeking soul
Are marked against attack
When history thunders by.
As so they stand, not knowing
That it is of no import
That their walls are still secure against time,
Nor seeing that they stand
No longer on horizons
And that the men who pass them by
Have objectives farther out
Across the plain and closer
To the sky.

Arthur Graham

For Teachers of the Free

The future is to the unfettered,
Those loosed from the tentacles of the past
And the heavy weight of lifeless idols,
Free for the march.
For the journey is always to the strong,
Those trained for rough terrain
Where only sun and star are friends
And wind and rain accent the new-found joy.
These give praise for the few shelters of life
To others who taught courage, not fear;
Who instilled wonder, pointed to the inner guide,
Then walked a bit along the way
To see, like Moses,
The Promised Land from mountain height
And watch from afar the entry of the chosen ones
And know in truth they are his sons.

Arthur Graham

The Wish and the Motive

What shall we then say to ourselves
When, in the hour of solitude,
We discover the moral space
Between the wish and true motivation?
The Wish, the aimless desire,
Arising from the surface
Of the stagnant waters of what we are,
Compresses and suppresses us
And drives us like sightless worms
Back again beneath the rocks of sin,
Makes us crawl the rut-like paths
Ever further from the light.
The Motive — the incentive,
The voice still crying
Almost inaudibly in the wilderness —
Beseeches us to look out of ourselves
As from a quaking house;
To look far across the sands
Of dreams and shifting emotion
To where, upon the precipice of time,
The shadow of man bends o'er the summit.
This is the reflection of hope, and science —
As of the moon, coldly casting the dark image
But reminding that there is ever greater man
Between the precipice and the light.
This is Motive, then, and not the Wish
To make such shadows in the sun
And to look beyond the smitten light
Where man giants stride the earth.
This is what we say in our solitude.
It is a prayer. It is a prayer.

Arthur Graham

This Much of Truth

DON CARLOS

This much of truth is given all to see:
The strange and fatal likeness linking you and me.
'Tis wrongly said we're different, you and I —
That lands and oceans part us, mountains high;
That language raises barriers, creeds defy
The comradeship of races. Were this true,
Then little hope remains for me and you.
Nay, 'tis not truth that limits and confines
Our faiths and hopes in dogmas and in shrines,
That says, "Lo, God is here, and there is not,"
And chains the universe to one fair spot;
'Tis blinded men and selfish cannot see
That truth, God's gift to men, must make men free.
Yes, worship at your altar, while I bend
My knees where I see truth and beauty blend;
Yes, chant your hymns and light your altar-fires.
My spirit with your hymns and prayers aspires
And knows that, seeking beauty and the good,
We shall find them and truth in brotherhood.

Karl M. Chworowsky

Prayer to the God Within

This life awaits the simple verdict of my heart;
I need no firm imperatives beyond.
If I can teach my languid heart to sing,
Full-voiced, that life is high and fair —
What radiance shall I lack? My song
Will surely spur the dream to deed
And make the dimly seen horizon-rim flash bright.
O brightest music! fiery sunrise in the sky!

Then let me touch a taper in my heart
And kindle there a steady burning flame
Against the shadows, and emerge once more
Into the gladnesss of the dawn dayspring.
May I be startled by a sudden joy
To levels ever lifting o'er the last,
Enlivened by the lilt of circumstance,
And warmed at ancient hearth fires blazing anew.

That which I cherish I become. I learn,
From deeps that call to deepest inward need,
To make of wish the fact. I surge and soar
To elemental strength within,
Which flows with cosmic thrust, like waves
Flung up by comets hotly plunged
Deep in some spatial sea. So also rise,
O tides of hope! and buoyant lift and stir my soul!

Ford Lewis

Welcome Life

Not halting nor reluctant would we move
Along the way of living, in dark dread
Lest some transfigured moment rise to prove
Our deep capacity for glory dead.

Confronted by the fleeting chance to soar
Or fall, we would not safely face away,
But gladly risk the less to gain the more,
And win with zest or lose without dismay.

We welcome life; we take what it presents
And build a superstructure made of dreams —
Above the sheer necessity of sense —
To house the hope and promise man esteems.

We worship life; the value it provides
We gladly take, and just as gladly give.
We pray to life: may all its sweeping tides
Instill in us the mighty strength to live.

John G. MacKinnon

Star-born

Ye earthborn children of a star
Amid the depth of space,
The cosmic wonder from afar
Within your minds embrace.

Look out with awe upon the art
Of countless living things,
The counterpoint of part with part
As nature's chorus sings.

Behold the wonder you have wrought
Within your little time:
The knowledge won, the wisdom sought,
The ornaments of rhyme.

Seek deeper still within your souls
And sense the wonder there —
The ceaseless thrust to noble goals
Of life, more free and fair.

Ye earthborn children of a star,
Who seek and long and strive,
Take humble pride in what you are:
Be glad to be alive.

John G. MacKinnon

In Memoriam

We pray for words — the words that best can say
How kind a man he was, how great his heart,
With what integrity he played his part.
He walked amid the factions of his day,
Yet for himself chose no weak middle way.
The dignity of man: this was his art —
No one left out, no person set apart,
And faith in God's good kingdom come to stay.

To grieve would be his courage to deny —
But could we find his spirit, this would be
His true memorial. If we could see
His vision and the truths that he lived by,
Then could we know — thank God! — life's destiny
Can be triumphant, endless victory.

Roscoe E. Trueblood

16

The Interpretation

Theology

The task of theology is to show how the world is founded on something beyond mere transient fact, and how it issues in something beyond the perishing of occasion. ALFRED NORTH WHITEHEAD

Notes on Contributors

George G. Brooks is minister of the Adams Memorial Unitarian Church in Dunkirk, New York.

Frank M. Cross, Jr., is Hancock Professor of Hebrew and other Oriental Languages at Harvard University.

Arthur Foote is minister of Unity Church (Unitarian) in St. Paul, Minnesota.

Charles Conrad Forman is minister of the First Parish in Plymouth, Massachusetts.

Duncan Howlett is minister of All Souls' Church (Unitarian) in Washington, D. C.

David R. Kibby is minister of the Unitarian Church in Pittsfield, Massachusetts.

Norman Livergood is now working toward a Ph.D. in philosophy at the Graduate School of Yale University.

Samuel H. Miller is dean of the faculty of divinity at Harvard University.

Mary Lou Page is a member of the Unitarian Fellowship of Cedar Falls, Iowa.

Harry B. Scholefield is minister of the First Unitarian Church in San Francisco, California.

Philip Schug is regional director of the Southwestern Unitarian Conference and minister of the First Unitarian Church in San Antonio, Texas.

Ralph W. Stutzman is minister of The Church of the Unity (Unitarian-Universalist) in Springfield, Massachusetts.

Robert B. Tapp is Dockstader Professor of Theology at The Theological School of St. Lawrence University in Canton, New York.

Herbert F. Vetter, Jr., is minister of the First Congregational Parish in Milton, Massachusetts.

Outgrowing Our Heritage

by Ralph W. Stutzman

One of the painful experiences of life is growing up to the ripe old age of five or six or seven and outgrowing our childhood concepts — our belief in the Easter Bunny and Santa Claus and the other imaginative characters that make young life so wondrous. It is also painful when we reach the age of maturity and reason, and face the possibility of outgrowing our spiritual heritage. For the free liberal churches, this remains a constant painful experience because, as we leave one frontier behind, we automatically, by our very nature, seek out another. One of the frontiers now confronting Unitarianism and causing much anxiety within our circles lies within the question: *are Unitarians Christians?*

This of course is a question that those outside the Unitarian church have asked for years and years. For a long time, it seems, we didn't much care what others were saying about us. As long as we considered ourselves a liberal part of the Christian church, that was all that mattered. Then, in 1950, the Federal Council of Churches joined with a few other Christian organizations to form the National Council of Christian Churches, setting as their least common denominator of faith this statement in their preamble: "In the providence of God the time has come when it seems fitting more fully to manifest oneness in Jesus Christ as divine Lord and Saviour, by the creation of an inclusive cooperation agency of the Christian Churches of the United States of America . . ."

This "inclusive cooperation agency" excluded the Unitarian church by the statement, "oneness in Jesus Christ as divine Lord and Saviour." Not that some Unitarians could not agree with the statement, but the denomination could not speak for *all* its members, saying that we do adhere to the statement of faith. At any rate, this brought the problem to a point of tension within Unitarianism. Some Unitarians simply said, "All right, so we're not Christians . . . as long as we are what we are, that's all that matters." This was more than just "sour grapes." Many of our ministers had found through their seminary education that they were not really Christian in belief, no matter how far you stretched the definition; and furthermore, they didn't want to fool anybody, especially the Christians, by saying that they were.

Yet, in 1957, at our May Meetings, the official annual meeting of the Unitarian denomination, when it was voted to change the name of our official denominational magazine from the *Christian Register* to the *Unitarian Register,* such an uproar was made by those Unitarians who considered themselves Christians that there was some question as to whether the sky was falling. Especially was there unrest among the Unitarians in New England, where social stature seemed so important and where the loss of the Christian veneer seemed to be a loss of social stature.

This, then, is the question that faces us: Should Unitarians, by principles of faith, recognize themselves as Christians?

I'm sure that if you have been a Unitarian for any length of time and have let it be known, you have been engaged in a conversation something like this: "Oh, you're a Unitarian. Hummmmmm. Tell me, are Unitarians Christians?" Then you attempt to give an answer which you know in advance will not be very satisfactory. But you try: "Well, you see, the basis of Unitarianism is really freedom to believe as you wish. Therefore we have no creed or statement of faith concerning Jesus. However, there are some points of general agreement where our freedom has led us." If the questioner is still listening at this point, you clear your throat and go on. "If you mean by Christian one who sees Jesus as God incarnate, a part of the trinity, then Unitarians generally could not be called Christian. But if you mean by Christian one who follows the teachings of Jesus and tries to emulate his life, then we would consider ourselves Christian. After all, we do come out of the Christian heritage."

Is this somewhat the way you answered? Until recently this was the type of answer I usually gave. But then I had to rethink my position — one of the advantages of our kind of religious approach — and lately, when someone confronts me with the question, I answer somewhat in this way: "I can't speak for all Unitarians nor for the church I serve, since the basis of our faith is freedom of belief. But my personal beliefs exclude the possibility of my being a Christian."

Now, in order to give you my reasoning on this, I am going to break one of the first rules of homiletics. One of the first rules in the art of preaching taught at any seminary is: never preach your doubts! The obvious reasoning behind such a rule is that the members of your congregation have enough doubts of their own, without hearing yours. Never preach your doubts because you may break someone's faith. With the drive for a larger membership prodding any minister, he can't afford to do that. Consequently, much of the minister's scholarship and study of the scriptures is never brought to the congregation. To this extent, the congregation is not getting its money's worth.

Any ministerial student worth his calling certainly has doubts. With the great intellectual strides of our time in archeology, and in higher and lower criticism of the Bible, one can't help but have doubts, and it is from this mental struggle that a firm rational set of beliefs finally emerges.

Is Christianity valid for Unitarianism? I doubt it. Or, if you prefer that one not preach his doubts, then look upon what follows as scholarship.

May I take you back in history to a Danish theologian of a century ago, Sören Kierkegaard. This theologian has more clearly defined Christianity and the price one pays to be a Christian than any other theologian to date. Sören Kierkegaard claims that when man is living on his most serious level of existence and looks within himself, what he sees is untruth, alienation from God, sin. One would think that, since he is created in the image of God, if he looked deep enough within he would find God and ultimate truth. Not so! The deeper he probes within, the further he finds himself from God. Truth, then, must come from outside man and not from within. If man is to be saved, he must be saved from outside himself, since *he* does not have this power. The rut of sin is too deep for man to pull himself out. Even his free will he cannot use wisely enough to get out of this rut. God must intervene in history if the gulf between God and man is to be bridged. The more the individual tries to develop a relation with God while in this state of sin, the deeper is his sense of despair over his sin — especially as he grows in his knowledge of God's love.

Now, says Kierkegaard, God can bridge this gap in relations in one of two ways. God can either bring man up to the stature of God Himself, or God can lower Himself and become a man. To choose the former would ultimately destroy the relation God hopes to bring about. If God re-established man to a state as pure as that of God, it would be like a rich man marrying a poor servant-girl. The girl would be happy in her new luxuries for a while, but she finally would realize that the rich man condescended to her level for her. This would eventually lead to such dissatisfaction that the marriage would be unhappy. So God chose the other way — he chose to bridge the gap in relations by becoming man in the form of Jesus Christ.

But in doing this, God now has offended the minds of men. The offense to one's mind at such a concept is double edged. It is offensive for us humans to accept the claims of Jesus to be a God. *Any* man who claims this would be offensive to us. On the other hand, it is an offense to the mind to believe that God could and would become a man. Can eternity enter time? Can infinite God enter into finiteness? Our reason says this is absurd. The reason cannot accept the concept that God could become a man — and such a man, says Kierkegaard: a mere carpenter who ends up dying on a cross like a common criminal. Forget your little formulas for proving that Jesus Christ was God, for this concept runs counter to rational and historic proof. This paradox is never resolved or explained rationally. It is only the love of God that enables one to live with the paradox. If you would be a Christian, you must accept this paradox, this unrational truth and the tension within that this concept brings to one. In short, if you would be a Christian you must sacrifice your mind at this point in favor of faith. Sören Kierkegaard goes on to encourage one to make this leap of faith and accept this new relationship with God.

The main reason Kierkegaard wrote as he did a hundred years ago was to point out this tension, this sacrifice of the mind, this cost of Christianity to the Christians of his day. He condemned the state church of Denmark for hiding this offense from the people. The *teachings* of Jesus had been kept by the church. They were not offensive. But the sign of God in history — the God/Man, Jesus Christ — had been pushed under the thinking surface in order that men might become Christians painlessly. Thus Kierkegaard points to the whole crux of the Christian faith.

That is why the works of Sören Kierkegaard are being read so widely by seminary professors and students — and also why he is not mentioned more often from the pulpit. He put his finger on the sore spot of his day. He also hurts in our day. Today, whatever Christian ministers want their religion to be, they want it to be intellectually respectable. Yet orthodox Christianity will always, must always, remain an offense.

I read Kierkegaard's works for the first time during my senior year in seminary. From my freshman year in college, eight years before, I had thought the deep questions of religion would be answered reasonably, when I got to seminary, by professors who would have grappled with these issues. Seminary turned out to be a disappointment on that score, but it wasn't until my senior year, when I read Kierkegaard, that I really understood why. The other theologians I had read and listened to were always trying to answer these questions in semilogical systems, in rational apologetics that often didn't meet common-sense levels. As long as you accepted their premises, you could stay on the merry-go-round. But question the basic premise — question the God/Man concept, question the very nature of God as being personal — and no answers were rational. Then I read Sören Kierkegaard, who said that the answer does not lie in rational categories; that, in fact, truth is an offense to the reason. If Christianity can be reasonably presented, why do you need faith? I have yet to hear this from a popular Christian pulpit.

I sincerely wish that more ministers would recognize the implications of their faith, and that those who do recognize them would preach them, instead of passing Christianity off as simply living the life of a good citizen. Listen a moment to Kierkegaard: "In Christianity there is perpetual Sunday twaddle about Christianity's glorious and priceless truths, its sweet consolation; but it is only too evident that Christ lived 1800 years ago. The Sign of Offense and the object of Faith has become the most romantic of all fabulous figures, a divine Uncle George. . . . Christendom has done away with Christianity, without being quite aware of it. The consequence is that, if anything is to be done, one must try again to introduce Christianity into Christendom."[1]

Kierkegaard has as clear a definition of Christianity and the predicament of Christianity in society as any I have ever read. He made the challenge of the leap of faith quite clear — dramatically clear. I refused to leap. I concluded that Kierkegaard was one of the most truthful theologians I had read. I concluded that he was one of the greatest Christians that ever lived. I concluded that Kierkegaard was right in claiming that to believe the doctrine of the Christian church one had to sacrifice his mind. And I concluded that I could not be a Christian by definition of these requirements. This was somewhat embarrassing, considering that I was just completing eight years of study for the Christian ministry at the time.

God had given me this brain to use to its greatest potential. It may not be much, but I'm not going to sacrifice it. Nor do I believe that God is the kind of giver who comes along some twenty years later and wants back what he gave — the rational processes of the human mind.

You ask me if I, as a Unitarian, am a Christian. If you mean by that, do I accept Jesus Christ as God incarnate, I must say no, I am not a Christian. But if you mean by a Christian one who

---

(1) *Training in Christianity*, trans. Walter Lowrie, Princeton, N. J., Princeton University Press, 1944. Cited in *A Kierkegaard Anthology*, Robert Bretall, ed., Princeton, N. J., Princeton University Press, 1951, pp. 396-97.

accepts the teachings of Jesus and tries to emulate his life, then I must reply: I am still not a Christian.

If I accepted the second definition — that is, one who accepts the teachings of Jesus and tries to emulate his life — my doubts (or my scholarship) would lead me to ask, Which Jesus should I follow? For when I read the New Testament, I find many conflicting views of Jesus the man, and many conflicting teachings. The whole difficulty, of course, arises when we take the gospels as biographies of Jesus of Nazareth. They are not. Rather, they are primers for the newly converted Christians of the first and second centuries.

A modern pacifist says to me, "Look simply at the teachings of Jesus, and you will see that he too was a pacifist. He tells you to turn the other cheek. Love your enemies." But I, being the rebel Unitarian that I am, think immediately of other sayings of Jesus: "Do not think that I have come to bring peace but a sword. For I have come to turn a man against his father and a daughter against her mother . . . and a man's enemies will be in his own household. No one who loves father or mother more than he loves me is worthy of me." I think of how he lambasted the Pharisees and Sadducees and told them they were going to hell. I think of his making a whip of cords to beat the money-changers until they fled the temple courts. "Well," says my pacifist friend, "those passages were Semitic hyperboles, exaggerations of speech to stress a point." But how am I to judge whether the passages he cited are the exaggerations, or whether the ones I cited are the exaggerations — or both?

Another friend approaches me, this one of the Norman Vincent Peale school, which views Christianity as the modern success story. He says to me, "Be of good cheer. Didn't Jesus say, 'Ask and it will be given to you. Seek and you will find'?" But then I think of the more demanding expressions of Jesus: "If any man would come after me, let him take up his *cross* and follow me."

Then a fundamentalist friend stressing evangelism approaches me and says, "All you need to do is believe. Didn't Jesus himself say, 'I am the way and the truth and the life; no one comes to the Father, but by me . . . He who has seen me has

seen the Father,' and 'Believe in God; believe also in me'?"
Then my mind runs to a saying of Jesus that goes, "Not everyone
who says to me, 'Lord, Lord,' will enter the Kingdom of Heaven,
but he who does the will of my Father."

Then one of those "do-gooders" of the social-gospel school of
thought comes to encourage me to go into social action because
this was the will of Jesus. "Just look at the entire Sermon on the
Mount," he says to me. "Whatever you wish that men would
do to you, do so to them." And, "This I command you, that you
love one another." Then my mind turns to a passage in the
sixteenth chapter of Matthew: "Truly, I say to you, there are
some standing here who will not taste of death before they see
the Son of Man coming in his kingdom." And this leads me to
think that perhaps the ethic Jesus taught was an extreme ethic,
appropriate only during an interim period between the few years
of his ministry and the time when, he expected, the world would
come to an end and he would return in all his glory. The first
Christians thought this time would come very soon — so soon
that Paul had to write a letter to the congregation of one church,
telling them to come down from the mountaintop and go back to
work: the end wasn't coming *that* soon.

Even if I decide that I will be a Christian, meaning by that
that I will follow the teachings of Jesus and imitate his life, my
scholarship leads me to question. We ought to realize, of course,
that in accepting this definition we have stripped Jesus of divinity. Now he stands before us as a grand example of how a man
should live, and his teachings as the teachings of truth. But is
this the way men should live? I think the phrase in Genesis is
right: "It is not good for man to be alone." The natural thing
is to find a wife. Already I have drawn a line limiting the extent
to which I am willing to imitate the life of Jesus.

As to his teachings: certainly some of the best teachings ever
taught to men are attributed to Jesus. The insights of some of
his parables have no parallel. Yet I find his concept of God as a
Heavenly Father somewhat disturbing. Heaven is not as easily
located as it once was, and the Fatherhood of God is in such
anthropomorphic terminology that I have to say, "I doubt it."

Jesus evidently firmly believed in a heaven and a hell which I must question. I must also question the validity of the God Whom Jesus referred to as having such a wrath at sinners that they would end up gnashing their teeth. Many passages seem to point to a belief of Jesus that there was an underlying structure of good in the world that ultimately would win out. I have faith in goodness only when it can be implemented practically. In other words, turning the other cheek is, in some situations, a good way to get killed. If turning the other cheek were practiced by one nation when men of other nations did not accept the same code of ethics, good men, innocent men, would get slaughtered. Good is not so powerful by its inner quality that it cannot be beaten.

Now my Unitarian Christian friends say to me, "You have carried this to ridiculous extremes. Certainly we do not mean when we say that we will imitate the life of Jesus and follow his teachings that we will remain celibate, leave our families and set out to be itinerant preachers. What we mean is that we will live by the goals that Jesus seemed to preach and live by: kindness, concern, sensitivity, compassion." But this becomes no different from the goals of humanism — or better, of Unitarianism — or better still, of any of the great religions of the world. By the time you water down the life and teachings of Jesus to such generalities you have so undercut the term *Christian* that any good Jew is now a Christian by that definition.

If you intend to follow that which you accept as valid, good and true, why not call yourself a Follower of the Valid, the Good and the True, rather than a Christian. Christian, by the very term, reads something into the name that says more than simply a follower of Jesus. It is one who hopes to be like Christ. Notice the term *Christ*, not Jesus, for Christ is the title given to the special Son of God. The name Christian, then, must go back to something in the area of Sören Kierkegaard's definition. Therefore the National Council of Christian Churches has every right to set, as its limiting statement of faith, belief in Jesus Christ as divine Lord and Saviour — even as we have every right to say, "This we cannot accept."

It is true that we have come out of a Christian tradition, a Christian heritage. But now I think it is time for Unitarians to face the fact that we have *come out*. If you want to go back in, and if you can make the necessary mental sacrifice to go back in, there are definite social advantages for you. If nothing else, you won't need to be embarrassed again by having someone ask you, "Unitarians . . . are they Christian?" You will be freed of the pains of being an individualistic thinker, the pangs caused by the never-ending search for truth. I am of the conviction, however, that the *adventure* lies on the liberal frontier. And it is an important adventure.

Why is it important whether Unitarians identify themselves as Christians or not? Well, one of the reasons is that we are moving toward a world civilization, away from simply national cultures. If civilization lasts another ten years, the world is going to need a denomination like Unitarianism in the midst of the Christian Western world. The stronger we are, the more of a soothing influence we can be as our world continues to shrink. As the major religions of the world begin really to rub shoulders, men of foreign countries are going to find Christianity to have an obnoxious air of superiority, even as men of the Western world now let the people of other nations know that *they* of the foreign nations are inferior.

Arnold Toynbee's book, *An Historian's Approach to Religion*,[2] has as its theme the coming tension among the major religions of the world. Toynbee pleads that the adherents of the various faiths not make hasty judgments about other faiths but allow time to present evidence that all the religions are dealing, if not with the same answers, at least with the same questions. Is this not a foundation already expressed and implemented in Unitarianism — the sifting of the essential from the unessential for the good life, a viewing of all faiths for the truths they hold?

It is important that Unitarianism grow. If we want a worldwide fellowship in the future, we must be working now in the areas that will help bring it about. I believe that the Unitarian

---

(2) Arnold J. Toynbee, *An Historian's Approach to Religion*, New York, Oxford University Press, 1955.

church can be such a mediating influence, and that Unitarians, not only as Unitarians but as human beings concerned for the truth in all religions, can be a bridge between the Eastern religions and the Western religion. It is important for us to recognize that, though we are of Christian origins, we are not limited by our heritage.

But more important than the practical part we can play in the world of tomorrow is the truth involved in this issue today. It is not exactly cricket for Unitarians to use the name Christian, when by taking that title we rupture the historic significance of its meaning. If we see something truly matchless, unequaled in history, in Jesus of Nazareth; if we see a dimension of his life that is of a nature that no other man can ever reach; if there is a Christ aspect, a God-with-us aspect about him that is radically different and totally unique — then we should feel free to accept the name Christian. But if we accept the truths of Jesus as we would accept the truths of any outstanding religious leader, then we ought to be honest enough to let go of our claim upon Christianity. This growing issue within Unitarianism is important because truth is important.

We have dedicated ourselves to the discipleship of advancing truth. No other principle could be more solid as the cornerstone of any faith. No other principle is more adventurous, nor more demanding. The growing pains of advancing truth hurt from the dissolution of Santa Claus right up to the insights gained on the day we die. Yet with the pain there is the satisfaction of having spent a life the way life was meant to be lived — in a continual acceptance of emerging truths; on the growing edge of God's evolutionary insights; as a pioneer, filled with fear and trembling, yet knowing that even if all else is wrong, our way of openness must be right!

American Unitarianism and Christianity

by Harry B. Scholefield

A recent sermon preached by the Reverend Ralph W. Stutzman, then Assistant Minister of All Souls' Church, Washington, D. C., has attracted nationwide attention. The sermon subject was "Outgrowing Our Heritage." Mr. Stutzman advanced the thesis that, though the Unitarian denomination had originated in the Judeo-Christian tradition, the time has now come to recognize that we have moved beyond that tradition. "It is true," he says, "that we have come out of a Christian tradition, a Christian heritage. But now I think it is time for Unitarians to face the fact that we have *come out.*"

I am impressed with the pertinence and timeliness of this sermon. That it touches on issues of real importance for Unitarians can be gauged by the variety of responses it has provoked. Some Unitarians agree with it completely; others are in just as complete disagreement.

I am also impressed by the fact that this issue discussed by Mr. Stutzman has been timely for more than one hundred years. Since the very date of the founding of the American Unitarian Association in 1825, we have been extremely self-conscious about our relationship to Christianity. Indeed, the major documents in our early history are concerned with this issue. William Ellery Channing focused on it in the Baltimore Sermon of 1819; Ralph Waldo Emerson was concerned with it in the beautiful Divinity School Address in 1838; and a few years later, in 1841, Theodore Parker addressed himself to it in his notable sermon "The Transient and the Permanent in Christianity." The issue has concerned the most thoughtful leaders of our denomination since its beginning. Obviously it admits of no easy solution. As it has caused concern and occasioned disagreement for so long a time in the past, we may be sure that it will not be settled definitively in the present or the immediate future.

I am impressed, finally, that Mr. Stutzman's contention —

as it applies, not to individual Unitarian churches or to individual Unitarians, but to the denomination as a whole — is basically correct. A text from the Book of Isaiah comes to mind: "The bed is shorter than that a man can stretch himself on it, and the covering narrower than that he can wrap himself in it." It is difficult for me to see how the word "Christian" can any longer be stretched to the point where it covers with accuracy the nature and purposes of our Unitarian denomination *as a whole.* I disagree with the thesis that individuals in the Unitarian church should no longer call themselves Christian. This is a denial of the "free mind principle" so basic to Unitarianism. I agree, however, that insofar as our denomination is concerned, the term Christian is inaccurate from any one of several points of view.

I should like to set this question in a broad historical perspective. Let us review a very significant chapter in American Unitarian history. In 1865, at the conclusion of the Civil War, a conference of immense importance for Unitarians was held in New York City. The inspiring genius of this conference was the Reverend Henry W. Bellows, Minister of All Souls' Unitarian Church in New York City. The purpose of the meeting was to bring together a large group of Unitarians who would seek methods of transforming the Unitarian denomination, which was at that time weak and ineffectual, into an effective instrument for the nurturing and spreading of liberal religion.

It became apparent even before the delegates assembled that there was, within the denomination, a profound difference of opinion as to what the aims and purposes of the Unitarian denomination were and how these aims and purposes should be described. Long before the conference met, there was widespread discussion which revealed divergent views. A conservative group believed that the primary allegiance of the Unitarian denomination should be to the Christian tradition. They felt that its main task was to diffuse the principles of Christianity, by which they meant the principles of liberal Christianity as they interpreted them. The "radicals," as they were called, felt that the primary allegiance of the Unitarian denomination should be to the principle of individual freedom of belief. Within the denomination there should be room for those who prized above all else the traditions of Christianity. There also should be room for those who derive their inspiration from other sources. There were set forth in that controversy, which is now more than one hundred years old, basic disagreements which have never been fully resolved.

As often happens, it was around a preamble — the preamble to the proposed National Conference of Unitarian Churches — that the disagreements crystallized. Delegates to the New York City conference, chiefly concerned with problems of organization, adopted a preamble which stated clearly that the members of the conference were disciples "of the Lord Jesus Christ, dedicated to the advancement of his kingdom." This phraseology, acceptable to the conservatives, was of course not acceptable to the radicals. Prolonged discussion of the question was postponed until the next meeting of the conference, scheduled to be held the following year in Syracuse, New York.

When the conference assembled for the second time in 1866, the distinguished Unitarian minister, Francis Ellingwood Abbot, leader of the radicals, arrived at Syracuse with a substitute preamble. He distributed copies of this preamble to the members of the conference in order to make certain that the issue would be discussed on the floor and not shelved by the Organizing Committee. (It appears that the Unitarians of that day — and perhaps in this respect they are not dissimilar to their descendants — would sometimes find ways of shelving issues to avoid free and open discussion.) The alternative preamble presented by Abbot asserted "that the object of Christianity is the universal diffusion of Love, Righteousness and Truth." It stated that nothing in the Christian position, if it were accurately set forth, could rule out the right of individual freedom, because "perfect freedom of thought is at once the right and duty of every human being." Stow Persons (whose book *Free Religion,* published by Yale University Press in 1947, is the chief source of historical material for this article), states that Abbot's preamble defines Christianity "as a practical ideal rather than as theoretical dogma, and the basis of its organization is 'Unity of spirit rather than Uniformity of belief.' "

To make a long but extremely significant story short, the Syracuse meeting adopted the "orthodox" preamble. Stow Persons writes that the conclusive argument was offered by James Freeman Clark "who feared that removing the 'Lordship of Jesus' from the preamble might be construed by the religious world as hauling down the Christian flag." When the question was put to a vote, the Abbot amendment was decisively rejected. "The Unitarians were determined to remain within the Christian fold, convinced that spiritual submission to Jesus in no way involved infringement of individual liberty, yet many of those who stood by the denomination did so with heavy hearts."

An important new development now took place. The radicals formed a new organization, calling it The Free Religious Association. It was organized to stimulate greater freedom of belief than either the National Conference of Unitarian Churches or the American Unitarian Association encouraged. Fortunately, most of its leaders never left the Unitarian denomination. It served to leaven the Unitarian lump. For a time, it, rather than the National Conference of Unitarian Churches or the American Unitarian Association, nourished the spirit of unfettered liberalism which we like to consider an outstanding characteristic of our kind of religious fellowship.

The Free Religious Association was organized on May 30, 1867. Its stated purposes were "to promote the interests of pure religion, to encourage the scientific study of theology, and to increase fellowship in the spirit." The first man formally to join the organization by paying his one dollar dues was Ralph Waldo Emerson. Among those who attended and addressed its first meeting were Emerson, John Weiss, Robert Dale Owen, William H. Furness, Lucretia Mott, Henry Blanchard, T. W. Higginson, D. A. Wasson, Isaac M. Wise, Oliver Johnson, F. E. Abbot and Max Lilienthal.

For the next fifteen years this controversy, which centered on the issue of individual freedom of belief within the Unitarian denomination and the relationship of the denomination to Christianity, was carried on with varying degrees of intensity. Then, in 1882, an amendment was added to the Constitution of the National Conference which, in a negative fashion, affirmed the principle of freedom of belief, giving it precedence over commitment to any specific set of religious traditions. The amendment stated that there is no authoritative test of Unitarianism and that those "who, while differing from us in belief, are in general sympathy with our purposes and practical aims" would not be excluded from the Unitarian denomination.

In the present bylaws of the American Unitarian Association, as revised and adopted in 1951, we see the results of the struggle which took place in our denomination a hundred years ago. It is worth recalling certain sentences in these bylaws. The American Unitarian Association is to "be devoted to moral, religious, educational and charitable purposes." In accordance with these purposes, it shall "diffuse the knowledge and promote the interests of religion which Jesus taught as love to God and love to man. . . ." Then there occurs, in the second section of the bylaws, the negative statement of the positive free mind principle: "The Association recognizes that its constituency is congregational in policy and that freedom of belief is inherent in the Unitarian tradition. Nothing in these purposes shall be construed as an authoritative test." I would add only that this qualifying statement is a part of the bylaws, not only of the American Unitarian Association, but also of many individual Unitarian churches.

I am, of course, using this important chapter in our denominational history for illustrative purposes. The same discussion which was carried on in the midnineteenth century goes on today. The same two positions are held throughout our denomination. The disagreement continues to appear at our annual meetings when we are concerned with phraseology or symbols that stem from our relationship to Christianity. It was manifest at the meetings of the American Unitarian Association in May 1957, when the name of our denominational monthly magazine was changed from the *Christian Register* to the *Unitarian Register*. It was emphasized even more strikingly at the Fourth Biennial

Convention of the Unitarians and Universalists meeting in Syracuse in October 1959. The most strenuous debate at this conference, as had been the case in the same city ninety-three years earlier, centered on the issue of the relationship of Unitarians to Christianity. The delegates overwhelmingly adopted, as part of a proposed plan to consolidate the two denominations, a statement of purposes and objectives that would have been considered extremely radical in 1866.

The bitterness and anxiety which marked the controversy in the 1860s have been largely dissipated. Yet the two positions widely held today are surprisingly similar to those held by Henry W. Bellows and Francis Ellingwood Abbot — although no one now wishes to raise a standard quite as conservative as that implied in the phrase "the Lordship of Jesus Christ."

Today's conservatives believe that Unitarianism is concerned to reinterpret Christianity and to diffuse more widely the principles of Christianity understood in the terms of liberalism. They grant that there is room in the denomination for men and women who are not Christian in their orientation. Still, the denomination's most important task, as they see it, is to interpret Christianity in terms of thought categories which will make it acceptable to thinking men and women today.

Today's radicals feel that the primary mission of the Unitarian Church is to establish a religious society dedicated to the principle of the free mind and to an acceptance of ethical values as the primary criterion of the meaning and depth of religious experience. The radicals acknowledge that American Unitarianism may always be linked in a distinctive sense to the Judeo-Christian tradition, because this tradition is the household of faith in which the denomination was born and in which it has grown. They would, however, acknowledge no one tradition — except that of the free mind principle — as being uniquely authoritative.

I myself hold the radical point of view. I believe that Emerson and Abbot were right. I believe that the directions staked out by the Free Religious Association are the directions in which our future lies. I think this is a broader direction, more closely

suited to the needs of our times and the needs of the future, than
the direction chartered by those who wrote the conservative preamble to the National Unitarian Conference which was accepted
by a majority of the delegates in 1866.

As I seek a better understanding of contemporary Unitarianism, I find myself making certain assumptions. American Unitarianism, like Unitarianism on the continent of Europe and in
England, came to life and grew in the liberal stream of the
Judeo-Christian heritage of the Western world. For a long time
to come, it will derive its major sustenance from Judeo-Christian
sources. The myths of Judaism and Christianity, the moral
earnestness of the prophets from Moses to Jesus, the writings in
the Old and New Testaments — these will continue to represent
links to the past which are essential to us as we live in the present. Rootless religion is virtually a contradiction in terms.

So also with the ancient holy days, such as Christmas and
Easter: they will continue to be celebrated by Unitarian churches
in ways that are consonant with contemporary thought. Paradoxically, they will also be celebrated in ways more consonant
with the pre-Christian meaning of these festivals than with doc-
trinally "sound" Christian interpretations. Ancient rites, such
as baptism, will continue to be used in a reinterpreted fashion.
So with other patterns of worship — the singing of hymns, the
use of readings, the practice of prayer or meditation. So far as I
can see, we shall be linked through these practices and usages for
a long, long time with our Judeo-Christian heritage. However,
I make the assumption that this may not always be the case.

I see our Unitarian churches placing the positive values of
the Judeo-Christian heritage in a new frame of reference which
makes the name Christian inapplicable to the denomination as a
whole. In this frame of reference, devotion to other values —
which are rooted in traditions much broader and much older
than even the Judeo-Christian stream — takes precedence over
devotion to Christianity.

What is it that differentiates us most strikingly from our
Christian and our Jewish brethren? John Weiss, one of the
Unitarians who spoke at the first meeting of the Free Religious

Association, stated the major difference. He said that in other religious groups, devotion to an article of faith set forth in creedal or doctrinal form is most important; whereas in ours, the method of seeking religious truth, and not the article of faith itself, constitutes our bond of unity.

I assume that contemporary Unitarianism is distinguished by its adherence to three primary values, none of which is uniquely Jewish or Christian in its origin. The first is devotion to that principle of individual freedom of belief which in Christianity is often more honored in the breach than the observance. One of the greatest scandals in Christianity, even now, is its spirit of dogmatic intolerance. The second value is the acceptance of ethical living — both individual and social — rather than creedal statements as religion's primary concern. The third value, which is steadily growing in importance, is not easy to name. Traditionally we call it worship. Albert Schweitzer calls it "reverence for life." Julian Huxley sees it as the mainspring of religious feeling and calls it "the sense of the sacred." Albert Einstein described it as wonder in the face of life's mysteriousness and regarded it as the source of science and of art as well as of religion.

Our devotion to ethics as a basic concern of religion, and to worship or wonder as the heart of religious experience, prevents our devotion to the free mind principle from being merely a rational exercise unrelated to the emotional side of our natures.

I believe that, in our future development, individual freedom will be conceived more as a means to an end than as an end in itself. Like Martin Buber, we shall see freedom as "a foot-bridge not a dwelling-place . . . the run before the jump, the tuning of the violin, the confirmation of that primal and mighty potentiality which it cannot even begin to actualize."[1] I believe that, as we grow wiser, we shall be less concerned with being free for the sake of being free and more concerned with the use of freedom for the fuller attainment of the joys of worship and wonder, of self-realization and of service to the great ideal

---

(1) Martin Buber, *Between Men and Man*, trans. by Ronald Gregor Smith, Boston, Beacon Press, 1955, p. 91.

of the dignity of man. I believe that the Unitarianism of the future will be increasingly humanistic, in the sense that it will be rooted in our faith in the dignity of man and man's capacity to use freedom for high ends. The kind of humanism I envisage will be most inclusive: it will flower into theism of many varieties and into reverent agnosticism. It will occasionally flower into that severely ethical atheism which might be described as Puritanism without belief in God.

I assume that, in a world in which traditions are shrinking and nationalism is becoming obsolete, Unitarianism will become more genuinely international than it has ever been in the past. I assume that the International Association for Liberal Christianity and Religious Freedom is but a tiny indication of what is to come in the form of a worldwide fellowship. It is also possible that, beginning with a merger with the Universalist Church of America, American Unitarianism will have to give up its own denominational label as evidence of its devotion to the Church Universal. The American Unitarian churches in the Judeo-Christian tradition may someday represent but a small fraction of the membership of a liberal church that is truly worldwide in the scope of its fellowship and in the reach of its organization. This church, stretching across the boundaries of nations and of sectarianism, would have its roots in the traditions of all the world's living religions, not exclusively or even primarily in the Judeo-Christian heritage.

With respect to diversity of patterns of worship, I assume that we have hardly begun to approach the degree of diversity long implicit in our fellowship, even within its American limits. We seem to forget at times that the free mind principle cuts in many directions. If fully utilized, it will promote the growth of a deeper conservatism, as well as a wiser liberalism or radicalism. I assume that there will always be in our fellowship individual churches (like the historic King's Chapel in Boston) using a prayer book as an aid to worship and endeavouring to combine the esthetics of Christian liturgy and the teachings of ethical Christianity with the principle of individual freedom of thought. I suspect that, in the future, many more Unitarian Churches will find new riches in the ancient traditions and teachings of Judaism and Christianity. Like Emerson they will bring fresh insights to bear upon the meaning of the life and gospel of Jesus of Nazareth. They will find in the depths of the Judeo-Christian tradition insights which will strengthen their faith in human dignity and reason.

I expect that, at the other end of what might be called the free mind spectrum, the newest and most progressively rebellious of our Unitarian groups will make their contribution. In these groups, the use of the word "God" or the use of such a discipline as prayer might be regarded as evidence of medieval obscurantism. Still, if they are founded on devotion to those values which are at the center of our life, they will in their own way contribute much to the diversity and the richness of the whole.

Between these extremes, there will be churches so broadly theistic and humanistic that it will be difficult to categorize them. All of these churches will contribute in their own way to the process of leavening the Unitarian lump and, by varied modes of worship and celebration, will open up new vistas and horizons.

My seven-year-old daughter and I have lately been enjoying together the ancient cycle of the moon. A few nights ago it was a thin, silver curve in the sky; gradually it approaches a full-orbed state. I assume that our Unitarian fellowship at the present time is at the very beginning of its cycle: it has a long way to go before its brightness is full.

Some persons may fear that, if Unitarianism develops as I have prophesied, it will prove as short-lived as the Free Religious Association. Some may fear that with this much diversity there can be little unity of the spirit. And some may fear that a religious fellowship thus oriented to the future will become formless and eclectic, and will cut all connections with its life-giving heritage. These, I admit, are real dangers. But they seem to me less threatening than the danger that we shall focus so narrowly on preserving our links with the past that we shall not be attuned to the new needs of a new age.

I believe that the words William Ellery Channing wrote in 1841 — only sixteen years after the formation of the American

Unitarian Association — depict the major danger to our kind of denomination. He was writing, in that year before his death, to his illustrious contemporary, the English Unitarian, James Martineau. "Old Unitarians," Channing said, "must undergo important modifications or developments. Thus I have felt for years. It began as a protest against the rejection of reason — against mental slavery. It has pledged itself to progress as its life's end, and now we have a Unitarian orthodoxy."

The need of our times is for a church which exalts the primacy of reason and ethics in religion, and exalts the sense of wonder and reverence in the face of the myriad facets of life's mysteries. It seeks the good in all religions and in all aspects of human creativity. It knows full well the rich relevance of the past and the high value of bright traditions, but it also knows full well that yesterday's wisdom does not necessarily contain the answers to today's questions. Its deepest commitment is to progress; and in the fulfillment of this commitment, it recognizes at all times the need for new concepts, new language and new and daring ventures of the human spirit.

Christianity and the Unitarians

by Duncan Howlett

Some Unitarians have recently attracted nationwide attention by declaring that they are not Christian. As a result, the impression is growing that the Unitarian denomination seeks to move beyond Christianity into "Universal Religion." I believe this impression to be erroneous. It is false in point of fact, and it is invalid as a statement of purpose.

First let us turn to the factual situation. That Unitarians are not Christian is an old and familiar charge. It has been hurled at us from the beginning by well-meaning defenders of the faith. Unitarians, for example, are not members of the National Council of Churches or the World Council of Churches. Nevertheless, most Christians have been content that we should live and preach our faith as we understood it, and have not tried to relegate us to a non-Christian limbo. Unitarians are members of and are active in state and local councils of churches.

Traditionally the Unitarians have been a liberalizing force in Christianity. Many of their teachings, once rejected throughout Christendom, are now generally accepted. What is called biblical criticism is a case in point. The technique of ferreting out information about Bible origins, authors, dates, manuscripts, purposes and all the rest, the development of which began in Europe in the early nineteenth century, was first accepted and brought to this country by the Unitarians. Following the Unitarian lead, the technique was eventually adopted by most of Protestantism, a fact which many a non-Unitarian is glad to acknowledge. The Unitarians led in popularizing the doctrine of mutual tolerance and understanding among differing religious points of view. They were the spearhead of the liberal movement, which by the 1920s had become the proud position of almost all Protestant leaders.

Protestantism has now abandoned the liberal point of view in favor of what is commonly called "neo-orthodoxy." The

41

broadly tolerant outlook that prevailed a generation or more ago has yielded to a resurgent demand that Protestant Christianity return to the ancient doctrines and creeds of the church. This is often given as a reason why Unitarianism should reaffirm its place in the Christian tradition. A liberal voice is needed now more than ever, it is said. Therefore the Unitarians should continue in their traditional role as spokesmen for liberal Christianity. Such arguments are not to be relied upon, however. If the Unitarian movement is to fulfill its true destiny, it must be what it has to be by virtue of its commitment to the truth-seeking process. We must not deceive ourselves. Mere utility is not an argument in the realm of truth. The Unitarians cannot be shown to be Christian or non-Christian simply because they or anyone else think that liberalism is needed in Christianity.

Our question is far more profound. Are those Christians right who declare that the Unitarians are not Christian in point of fact? In attempting to answer this question, it is worth noting who makes the charge and why. Generally speaking, only the theologians would exclude the Unitarians from Christianity, and they have always had the disagreeable habit of excluding people, even each other. They draw apart into separate churches, set up their own definitions of Christianity and declare that all who do not conform to the formulas they have chosen are not Christian at all. The practice is as widespread as it is invidious, and as exasperating as it is arbitrary.

The Unitarians have never been willing to accept a definition of Christianity that excluded them. They have insisted that Christianity is not narrow, but broad; that Christ's commandments for men were inclusive brotherhood and inclusive worship of God. On the whole, the Unitarians have countered the charge, not so much by argument, as by preaching and practicing Christianity as they understood it. This for them has been synonymous with the highest form of religion that man has yet attained.

Unitarians have always claimed a rightful place in Christianity because every factual, nondoctrinal definition places them squarely in the midst of it. Historically, sociologically, psychologically, morally and spiritually they are and have always been Christian. And so they may be shown to be theologically also, provided the right to define Christianity is not surrendered in advance. No man and no church may exclude another from Christianity. This has always been a basic tenet of the Unitarian faith.

And now we behold the Unitarians themselves joining with the very most orthodox in saying that Unitarians are not Christian. It is as if, mistaking the accusation for the fact, they accepted it and declared it to be the very truth. Emphasizing the differences between themselves and the main body of churches, the "non-Christian" Unitarians seek to separate the denomination from Christianity by public declarations of independence. Oddly enough, narrow definitions of Christianity of the sort that Unitarians have always objected to are frequently given as the reason for the proposal.

Thus we find our "non-Christian" Unitarians, usually the most vociferous in pointing out what they believe to be erroneous in Christian thought, arguing from definitions of Christianity devised by the most orthodox. Often these are definitions which many an avowed Christian would not accept either. It is curious that those who are most sharply critical of Christianity should be the only Unitarians willing to accept a narrowly theological definition of it. It is especially difficult to understand when we realize that, from the strictly factual point of view, Christianity is one of the most fundamental aspects of western culture. For this reason, one would expect that independent-minded men and women would prefer a descriptive and factual, rather than a theological and apologetic definition.

A more significant question rises here, however, that cannot so easily be disposed of. Quite apart from whether Unitarians are or are not Christian in fact, what should be their aim? Should they give up their place in Christianity voluntarily, and publicly declare themselves to have embraced "Universal Religion" in its stead? Should they strive to become a supra-Christian, supra-Buddhist, supra-Jewish, supra-Mohammedan religion? Suppose that by successive declarations of independence and by withdrawal from participation in councils of churches and other activities, by changing their worship, their hymnody, their holidays and their language — if they were able successfully to do all these things, what would they accomplish? Could they move beyond Christianity in fact, and would they then be able to establish what men would recognize to be "Universal Religion"?

If the idea were valid, the Unitarians would have adopted it long ago, for it has been debated in the denomination from the beginning. William Ellery Channing declared himself to be a member of the "Universal church." "The soul breaks scornfully these barriers, these webs of spiders," he wrote, "and joins itself to the great and good; and if it possesses their spirit, will the great and good cast it off because it has not enrolled itself in this or another sect? Virtue is no local thing. It is not honorable, but for its own independent and everlasting beauty. This is the bond of the Universal church: no man can be excommunicated from it but by the death of goodness in his own breast."[1]

Channing, of course, never advocated cutting the ties between Unitarianism and Christianity. The idea would have been unthinkable to him. Unitarianism was to him an expression of Christianity, the truest expression possible. Some of today's proponents of Universal Religion would, if they were consistent, have to argue that he was afraid to abandon Christianity, or that he had not attained sufficient maturity to be able to do so, for they have often leveled such accusations at their opponents.

The role of Unitarianism in Christianity has been under constant debate among Unitarians ever since Channing's time. During the period following the Civil War, a controversy of denominational proportions developed over the issue, and it continued for years. Now it is coming to the fore again. As Channing saw, there is a sense in which Universal Religion is implicit in the Unitarian position. Then, it is argued, if this be the case, let us cut our ties with Christianity and boldly declare for Universal Religion. In no other way shall we be able to fulfill our manifest

---

(1) Quoted by A. Powell Davies in *America's Real Religion*, Boston, Beacon Press, 1949, p. 51.

destiny. There is an inner logic in our movement that impels us inexorably in this direction. So the argument runs.

But there is a fallacy in this reasoning which our denominational leaders have always recognized and labored to point out. Because this fallacy is not immediately apparent, it has to be pointed out to each successive generation of Unitarians. Briefly stated, it is this: to cut our ties with Christianity and set ourselves up as a church of Universal Religion is to give up our role as liberals and to substitute for it a separate sectarian existence. This may sound incredible, and yet it is true.

We deceive ourselves with words. The Roman Catholic church claims to be universal. That is what the word catholic means. For this reason, many Protestants claim the right to call themselves catholic also. Various Protestant churches think of themselves as universal. What is the United Church of Christ? What is the ecumenical movement? Do the proponents of "Universal Religion" think that 100,000 Unitarians are in fact more universal than these?

It is argued that we, in contrast with all others, are truly universal because our beliefs are universal, while others are narrow, exclusive and sectarian. Yet who, besides ourselves, says so? Does our church become universal by our asserting that it is? To make such a claim is only to enter the sectarian clamor, where mutually conflicting claims to universality drown each other out. It is to establish our movement upon a dogma. A dogma is a religious truth propounded by the church that accepts it, and declared to be true because that church avows that it is. Non-dogmatic truth is established in an open encounter of mind with mind in the marketplace. Any claim to universality that we make will remain a dogma until recognized authorities in the matter, not members of our group, are willing to declare that we have in fact achieved universality.

But we have arrived at Universal Religion by this very kind of encounter, say the proponents of "non-Christian" Unitarianism. So say all the claimants to universality, each the self-proclaimed arbiter of the truth of its claim. That is dogma. It shifts the burden of proof from you to your opponent. Unitarians have heretofore always accepted the burden of proof for every article of their faith.

Neither the Unitarians nor anyone else will attain Universal Religion merely by declaring themselves to be in possession of it. In the end it will be the historians and not the theologians, Unitarian or otherwise, who will decide this question. It is one thing to challenge Christianity in the name of its own highest teaching, as the Unitarians have always done. It is quite another to set yourself up as holier than thou, and to withdraw from Christianity as if it were beneath you.

Am I then saying that no objectors may ever separate themselves from their parent body without thereby becoming dogmatists? Cannot a separated sect be a nondogmatic sect, animated by complete open-mindedness? The answer to this question is, of course, yes. Christianity itself came about as a result of such a separation. So too did the Reformation. The dogmatism came later. Unitarianism resulted from a similar separation, and to date has kept itself free from dogma.

There is a significant difference here that we must not overlook. In each of these cases, the separation came as a result of the action of the parent body. In these classical instances, the parent body first sought by force to compel the reform movement to conform. Failing this, they then disavowed it. But who, since the days of Jedidiah Morse a hundred and fifty years ago, has sought to make the Unitarians conform to Christian orthodoxy? In fact, down through the 1920s the tendency was all the other way. During this period, as we have seen, Protestantism, far from trying to force conformity upon the Unitarians, slowly moved toward the Unitarian position.

For parallels to the present demand for the separation of Christianity and Unitarianism, we look not to the long history of religion, but to the nineteenth and twentieth centuries in which several experiments in world religion have been attempted. One was the Free Religious Association, a protest movement that had its origin in Unitarianism. Another is the Vedanta movement, of Indian origin. The Ethical Culture Society might well be included in such a list also. None of these groups was driven out of the larger traditional religious group in which it had its origin. These were voluntary separatists. Each, without persecution, withdrew to form a new society in the name of a higher and more universal principle than that expressed by the parent body.

To stress the fact that one religious group withdrew from the parent body voluntarily, while another was forced out, may seem at first like a distinction without a difference. In fact, in certain specific instances, it might well be difficult to tell whether a group withdrew voluntarily or was forced out. The difference is fundamental, however, because it relates to the beliefs and practices of the separating group; and these, of course, are the heart of any religious society. The crux of the matter is that the separatist group takes with it the body of beliefs and practices of the parent body, modified in accordance with a principle that both acknowledge, but which they apply differently. Jesus and the group that formed in memory of him at Pentecost were not separatists from Judaism. They meant to purify Judaism in accordance with its own precepts. That the Jerusalem gathering soon departed from this ideal is another matter. The point is that they began there, and that is why we can with accuracy today speak of the Judeo-Christian tradition.

It was the same with Luther. He had no intention of breaking with the single Christian Roman church of the West that existed in his day. Finding himself forced outside it, he nevertheless continued to think of himself as Christian. In fact, Luther thought of himself as leading a movement that was more truly an expression of the Christian ideal than the great church of Rome itself. That is why Protestantism is Christian. And it was the same with the Unitarians. They also were forced out, although they believed themselves to be moving toward a fuller and better Christianity than existed in their time. Many other instances of this principle might be cited from the religious history of men, but these should suffice to make the point.

It is important to notice that, in each of these cases, the separating movement knew from the outset what it was and where it stood, because it continued to hold to the main body of traditions and practices of the parent group. Christianity in the first few centuries provides a perfect example of the principle. After its declaration of independence from Judaism, doctrinal controversies set in which were not resolved for hundreds of years. It is the very doctrines worked out in this period, after Christianity declared its independence of Judaism, to which the "non-Christian" Unitarians object most. Had Christianity continued in the spirit of Jesus to preach a refined and prophetic Judaism, "non-Christian" Unitarians would today find far less in it to object to than they do. This is true, not because it is Judaism, but because in prophetic Judaism, as brought to full and sharp focus in Jesus, they perceive the very universal principles that draw them toward what they call "Universal Religion" today.

The reformer who accepts what seems to him and to all men fundamentally valid in the religion of his culture is, however, saved from dogmatism. He does not become a dogmatist until he declares that his beliefs are right because some religion has officially declared them to be so. But if he rejects his own tradition and sets up in its place one that he himself declares to be valid, then he is in serious danger. In theory it would seem that he could do this and still remain open-minded, nondogmatic, nonsectarian and free. In point of fact he cannot.

A very real dilemma confronts anyone who tries to separate himself from the religion of his culture and embrace "Universal Religion" in its stead. What does a supposed world religion do in practice? On the one hand, if it is able to remain so free that all comers from all religions of man are welcome and can feel at home, how is it possible to give the movement either form or content? If a church is completely open-minded and has no doctrine of its own except a belief in one religion for all, then the movement stands empty, self-condemned by its own vacuity.

On the other hand, if such a movement seeks to give itself content, how does it do so? It must fabricate symbols of its own, beliefs, readings, practices — everything; or it must borrow from the elements already to be found in existing religions. Where the experiment has been tried, both methods have been used. Yet both have serious limitations. It is well established that truly meaningful symbols, formulas and usages in religion are evolved over a long period of time. In the nature of things they can rarely be fabricated satisfactorily. Furthermore, even a newly contrived and carefully designed usage may be satisfactory to some but quite unsatisfactory to others. Insofar as such devices are employed, they limit the freedom of those who dislike them or find them meaningless.

The problem becomes more acute when, in the effort to find content of expression for a world religion, borrowings from existing religions are made. Here symbols and customs are often not merely distasteful but emotionally objectionable, due to the intensity and bitterness that religious strife has often engendered down the centuries. Certain Hindu symbols, for example, might well be offensive to people of Mohammedan origin; certain Christian usages might be offensive to people of Jewish origin; while Buddhist views would not be congenial, let us say, to Shintoists.

A further problem besets anyone who appoints himself to the task of establishing a world religion. Insofar as concrete elements are stated and used in his organization, they constitute the belief and practice of a sect, and insofar as the members of the group claim that these beliefs and practices celebrate Universal Religion, just insofar have they embraced a dogma and exchanged their former freedom for sectarian servitude. It may be frustrating, but it is true. A little church or a big one, claiming to be above all others and to be an expression of Universal Religion, can amount to nothing more in fact than to being one of the many claimants to unique superiority among the religions of men — a claim which, in every instance, is supported by none but those who make it.

To try to detach ourselves from Christianity is to engage upon self-important sectarian folly. At best we shall succeed in becoming one more noble experiment in eclecticism. At worst we shall, like the Free Religious Association, end as a debating society, firmly believing in the common religion of all humanity, yet incapable of giving it form lest, in doing so, we impinge upon the individual's freedom to choose his own.

In the Unitarian church we have always feared above all

else the danger of falling into sectarianism. But we have always supposed that the threat of it lay in what is known as "Channing Unitarianism," because the attempt to peg the movement upon Channing's thought has repeatedly been made during the last century, and because orthodoxy always imposes itself upon a church out of loyalty to a great past.

Now, however, to our astonishment, just the contrary is the case. In the Unitarian church, where the doctrine of freedom is central, the danger of our falling into a sectarian orthodoxy apparently lies in the opposite direction. Our danger seems to be that we will adopt some particularist expression of religion, believing it to be a general principle. Our recent history shows that the most doctrinaire of our men are to be found more often among the advocates of a non-Christian rather than of an avowedly Christian Unitarianism. To date, however, we have successfully fought the dangers of fixing the movement in "Channing Unitarianism" or any other historical brand, and we have also successfully avoided fixing the movement in transcendentalism, free religion, humanism or theism. It is just as important to our future growth and our role as exponents of religious freedom that we do not now succumb to the siren voice of Universal Religion. Like all the other proposals that have been made to us, it sounds at first like the realization of our most implicit principles. But, like all the others, it turns out to be in fact a sectarian trap into which we must not permit ourselves to fall.

We have nothing to fear if we will face candidly the issues that lie before us. Unitarianism will not surrender its present substance and form in pursuit of an ideal that is either eclectic and sectarian or too lacking in content to be meaningful, if, in accordance with accepted practice, we examine every proposal dispassionately and on the merits of the case. We believe devoutly in all that Universal Religion wants to do, but we are practical-minded men and women, and we propose to move toward this ideal in a practical way. Until the Unitarians have found a better formula through which to express their convictions, they will remain squarely in the prophetic Judeo-Christian tradition, rebels against its ecclesiasticism, yet with their rebellion animated by allegiance to its highest prophetic insights.

Let us, as Unitarians, continue to proclaim the goal of a universal religion for all men in which each recognizes the validity of the approach of all. We ask only that every religion take its rise from honest conviction and that it be dedicated, not alone to the welfare of the self, but to the welfare of all men. Let us never cease to affirm that every man has a right to his own religion, and that the greatest folly we can commit is to think that we are better than other men. Nor should we with feigned humility declare ourselves to be worse.

Let us, as Unitarians, continue to direct the attention of men to the spiritual qualities and the moral precepts of Christianity — and of religions other than Christianity as well. Let us continue to insist that the worship, the scriptures and the beliefs of Christians are not all that is holy. Let us make increasing use of the elements of other religions in our churches, not alone for the validity they possess, but to demonstrate our belief in the underlying unity of all the religions of men.

On the other hand, let us not attempt to separate ourselves from Christianity as if it were unworthy of us. There is far more to Christianity than many a Unitarian apparently realizes. Our greatest danger here is ignorance. Few Unitarians give any indication that they are aware of the issues now being debated in orthodox Christianity. We need to know the work of men like Paul Tillich and Reinhold Niebuhr.

We have often denounced the thinking of the orthodox. We have flung epithets at them. But where among Unitarian thinkers do we find anything like a full-scale refutation of the present position of Protestant orthodoxy? Where is the man who meets argument with argument and point with point? Where, in fact, is the man in our midst who knows what the orthodox are driving at, and who is prepared to take up the theological argument at the point to which it has now been brought? Not unless we know what Christianity is, dare we declare that we have outgrown it. At the moment the danger may be greater that Christianity will outgrow us.

Let the Unitarians continue to preach their gospel of one world, one brotherhood of men, one truth and one Eternal Spirit rising in the hearts of all men everywhere. Let us continue along our present path, preaching the truth as we see it, using scripture that is an authentic utterance of the human spirit wherever we find it, employing such myths and symbols as may have true and genuine meaning for us, wherever they may be found, while, unhampered by tradition or any other authority, we seek the truth and give full and free expression to the upsurging of man's religious spirit.

Let us be Christian, if Christians we are, not because we conform to any of the creeds of Christendom, but because people can recognize in what we do and say an authentic expression of the true Judeo-Christian ideal. As for Universal Religion, let us not boast that it is ours; rather let us exemplify in our total denominational life so inclusive a spirit that others may be willing to make the claim for us. We cannot leap to the summit of the mount of religious unity. We shall arrive there at the last only if each of us in his own way climbs it himself with painful steps and slow. We shall avoid the sectarian trap if we lay claim to being no more than religious pilgrims of Christian origin and tradition, following the path of truth and light as we see it wherever it may lead. Let it suffice for us that we have found in the Unitarian church a company of like-minded men and women with whom we rejoice to join our hands and hearts in the unending pilgrimage of the human spirit.

In Love with God

by Philip Schug

Some time ago, one of our members phoned me and stated that she and her husband were taking instruction in the Episcopal church and were joining it the next Sunday. For three years or so they had been unable to attend our services with any real sense of satisfaction, and for two years had attended not at all. They were now finding the support they needed in this more orthodox church.

About a year ago, another of our members came to see me and to let me know that she was taking instruction in the Roman Catholic church, which she subsequently joined.

I know these three people well, and I feel they have done what is right for them. There is little doubt in my mind that their emotional needs, and their needs for direction, are better satisfied by the churches they have chosen. The young lady who joined the Catholic church stated explicitly that she was unable to give direction to her own life, that she needed to be told what is right and what is wrong; that as long as she was trying to struggle with these problems without authoritative direction, she made a mess of her own life, and that now she no longer needed to struggle; rather, she obeyed, and willingly. There is little doubt that these people consider themselves deeply in love with God. God, for them, is a loving Father — stern and demanding as regards his children, wrathful to those who do not accept Him or obey Him, yet loving and kind to those who believe and faithfully follow His directions. Their salvation is assured.

Albert Schweitzer, who is today widely acclaimed as the greatest living Christian, is also deeply in love with God. Schweitzer, however, does not think of God in terms that would be meaningful to these three people. To Schweitzer, God is a mystical experience, not something in which you believe or do not believe, not something (or someone) to which (or whom) you look

for explicit direction and consolation. Philosophically, he thinks
of God as impersonal Force. Mystically, he thinks of God in
terms of ethical Will. These two do not coincide, he admits, but
if he must put into words what he thinks and feels, this comes as
close as his modes of expression permit. And it is his feeling, not
his thinking, which predominates:

> This mystery, which I have experienced, is the decisive fac-
> tor in my thinking, my willing and my understanding. . . . My
> life is completely and unmistakably determined by the mysterious
> experience of God revealing Himself within me as ethical Will
> and desiring to take hold of my life.[1]

Now why is it that some people think of God in terms of a
Father Who commands one to accept particular articles of faith
and to follow explicit directions, while others think of God in
terms of impersonal Force and ethical Will? Why is it that some
people think of God as separate and distinct from them, while
others think of God as permeating all existence and coming to
fullness through them? And, we might ask, why is it that some
people never, or almost never, think of God?

Perplexing as these questions are, it is not difficult, in my
estimation, to get answers to them. But to get answers we must
begin with people, not with religious or theological systems.

Erich Fromm seeks the answers to questions such as these
in the development of the ability to love. The need to love, he
asserts, derives from our experience of separateness and the need
to overcome the anxieties resulting from separateness. These
anxieties push us toward union; and the religious form of love,
which may be thought of as the love of God, is not to be distinguished psychologically from these same experiences as regards
people. Being in love with God, he suggests, has as many different
qualities and aspects as being in love with some other person or
people.

To me such a clarifying thought is vastly significant, for
there is probably no one who does not sense, deep within himself,

---

(1) Albert Schweitzer, *Christianity and the Religions of the World*, New
    York, The Macmillan Company, 1923, pp. 77-78.

the need to love completely himself, some other and others. If being in love with God is not essentially different from being in love with humans, we have a beginning for understanding that can prove most fruitful. Let us, then, look into the question of what it means, humanly, *to love* — and so approach our problem of the love of God.

Let us first think in terms of what love is.

There will probably be no disagreement with the thought that love is an attitude or an orientation of character or personality. As an active process, love has to do with our relatedness to all things around us. Everyone of us probably has experienced the feeling of almost complete harmony and oneness with all things around him — the feeling that comes when all his worries and fears are pushed into the background and he is completely relaxed and at peace in his soul. At such times the grass seems to be greener than ever before, the sky more blue, the car more dependable, the dog more waggly-tailed, the children — even the neighbors' children — more angelic, and all the members of one's household and acquaintances more truly worthwhile people than we have usually thought. We feel more noble, more powerful and more worthwhile than at any other time. It is truly a high point of experience, and not a few of us have had to stifle the urge, which comes upon us at such moments, to hug and kiss everyone in sight. Life is wonderful under the power of love.

Now, if you have observed this in yourself, you will also have observed how indiscriminate are your feelings of love. You love everybody and everything. This is not to say that you are utterly without taste, and it is not to say that you make no distinctions. Your habitual reactions — and your caution, which helps you avoid pain — rather quickly assert themselves. A few simple frustrations, such as come when a friend says, "Phil, you must behave yourself," or the mailman delivers an extra large bill about which you had forgotten momentarily, are enough to jar you back into reality and take away some of the mystic experience of love. But for a deliciously extended moment, at least, you understood that love was a total orientation of the personality, and you understood that love was without exception and without limits. Love, in this sense, knows no object nor objects. You do not think of loving husband or wife, children or parents, friends or neighbors; indeed, you do not think of loving God. You think — or perhaps feel — that you love and are loved. You know, for a moment, that love is the most important thing in the world. You are love, or you are a part of it.

But people ordinarily do not live on this plane for an extended period of time. Rather soon, and for some it is very soon, most people come back into what they call "reality" and concentrate their attentions on specific objects. In a sense this is tragic, and in another sense it is necessary, for it is through the love of objects that we come to understand the meaning of love and exercise it as a creative activity. The mystic experience, which raises us far above the ordinaries of life, may be approached by way of the love of specific objects, though I doubt if it may be thought of as a generalization of the love of specifics. It is properly on a different plane, but that plane can probably never be reached without the ability to love specific people. Let us, therefore, turn to the objects of love.

First, those who are our equal are properly and commonly objects of love. "Fellow human beings" might be a better way of expressing this, for many of us are wary of that term "equal" after having examined it closely. Such love is usually known as brotherly love. It encompasses a sense of responsibility, care and respect for other human beings, the desire to further their lives and to help make them meaningful. Most of us develop and exhibit a love of equals because we recognize within other people a oneness with ourselves. They feel the same heat and cold that we do, the same sorrow and joy, the same hunger and pain. It sometimes takes a surprisingly long time for us to recognize this, and some of us never recognize it with regard to many other people around us, but practically all of us are able to recognize it in a few. When we do, there is a lessening of the desire to treat them as objects and a heightening of the desire to reach into their inner cores of being and know them directly and intuitively. As we extend our capacity to love one person in this way — first to several people and then to many — we approach the ability to love actively all people.

Second, those who are definitely not our equal but are less than our equal are also properly objects of love. Children are the most universally recognized objects of this nature. They cannot be our equal for many years after their birth, because of their utter dependence upon the active character of love on the part of their superiors. Without it they would soon die. This love of those who are definitely not our equal is often thought of in a two-fold manner as motherly and fatherly love. The difference has little to do with male and female, for either may exhibit both types of love so recognized; rather, it refers to conditioned and unconditioned love. Motherly love is thought of as unconditioned; that is, as wholly outgoing regardless of the nature or worthiness of the object. The object is loved completely, which means that it is totally aided to further its own ends, simply because it is. Fatherly love is thought of as conditioned, in the sense that it is outgoing only if the object of love merits it by exhibiting desirable qualities or being properly submissive. You will recognize theological overtones in this.

A third proper object of love which may clearly be distinguished from these two is one's self. Most of us will readily recognize that the self is not only a *proper* object of love but a *necessary* object of love. For the most part, we accept as axiomatic that one cannot properly love others if he does not at the same time love himself. This understanding of the necessary place of self-love has developed gradually as we have come to understand that love is *a capacity of the personality,* and thus essentially indivisible so far as external and internal objects are concerned.

Despite the wisdom locked in the biblical injunction "Love thy neighbor as thyself," it has seemed profitable for the directors of Western culture, who understand paternalistic love better than any other kind, to insist that self-love is the same as selfishness. We are developing beyond this understanding; and as we develop, paternalism is losing its grip, which suggests that some types of object love naturally war with other types. This is true not only in this specific instance but also when the love of an inferior is confused with the love of an equal. Many mothers and fathers, for example, in their confusion of understanding, try to love their children as equals, only to discover that under such circumstances the children get the best of them every time. A proper love of self is necessary for a proper love of others.

A fourth object of love, which is really a special case of the love of equals, is the love of those who are also sexual partners. Among some people, no equality of sexual partners is recognized; but when it is, the experience of love between the sexes may readily reach the mystic level and may often generate it. The feeling of complete oneness or complete union of spirit reached by some in sexual union banishes the anxieties of separateness and leads to the loftiest understanding of love we know.

Now I think it interesting that Erich Fromm does not discuss, nor even mention, the love of those who are not equal but superior. Logically we might assume that, if there can be a love of those who are not equal but inferior, there can — and must — also be a love of those who are not equal but superior. Rather, he goes directly to the love of God as an object, and shows that the love of God follows the same patterns of the emergence of love into conscious awareness.

The highest state of the love of God, suggests Fromm, is that of mystical union, in which all feelings of, and anxieties concerning, separateness are eliminated. The person who truly loves God is one with God. He does not think consciously of loving God, just as he does not think consciously of loving his neighbor or his children. He just loves. He is love: God is love: he is God. There is no difference. Those who have experienced human love in this way will have no difficulty with this development of the subject, and they will recognize the validity that is to be found in it.

There remains the question of why Fromm is silent regarding love of those who are not equal but superior. In our common understanding, is not God supposed to occupy this position? Are not those who seek to place themselves in submission to God, as one places himself (or is placed by circumstance) in submission to father and mother at the time of conception — are they not the people who *truly* love God? They claim they are, and most of us accept the claim at face value. If we are unable to place ourselves in the same position, we often feel that something is lacking in our lives that is supplied in the lives of those of simple faith. What is that void?

Might it not be that we are lacking not love but fear? Might it not be that we are lacking not love but dependency? We fear and need those who are not equal but superior, but it can hardly be said that we love them until we have an intuitive recognition of oneness or equality.

Fear and dependency are as far removed from love as east is from west, but men liberally use the coinage of love in the commerce of life. It is love, perfect love, which casts out fear; and it is love, perfect love, which casts out dependency. Yet fear and dependency may masquerade as love. When gilded with love, fear and dependency might be mistaken for love, but they are as counterfeit as would be a gilded brick in the vaults at Fort Knox.

We thus arrive at answers to our question: Why do some people think of God in terms of a Father who commands them to accept particular articles of faith and to follow explicit directions, while others think of God in terms of impersonal Force and ethical Will. We come to understand why some people think of God as completely separate from them, while others think of God as permeating all existence and coming to fullness in and through them. And we can know why some people never, or almost never, think of God.

He who knows no separation from God, because he has learned the essence of love, knows no fear, no dependency and no difference between himself and God.

The Third View

by David R. Kibby

Surely one of the most interesting features of life in the United States today is the preoccupation with religion that is everywhere apparent. Not long ago this preoccupation was hailed as a religious revival. Great numbers of people returned to the churches. Money poured into them. Expansion of facilities became necessary, and many attractive new churches were built. Religious books and movies gained immense popularity. Revivalists interested tremendous audiences. Even the average preacher was impressed by the fact of greatly enlarged congregations.

All this might well have passed for a revival of religion had not certain people noted, sometimes with surprise, that there seemed to be no correlative constructive impact on society of the kind that might be expected. The interest in religion seemed, by all odds, to be far more quantitative than qualitative.

But no one will deny that there has been a new interest in religion. What, then, has happened?

For the most part, this new interest has been channeled toward a re-emphasis on certain traditional forms and concepts. This reversion has not been accompanied by the critical evaluation of those norms and precepts that might seem indicated in the light of modern knowledge. Where there has been any critical evaluation at the higher echelons of religious scholarship, it has not been allowed to filter down to the level of the common man. Where it has begun at the lower levels, it has been promptly discouraged, suppressed or eradicated. In this regard the church has found itself in the role of the possessive and overprotective parent who, wittingly or unwittingly, imposes a childlike level of development so that dependence and obedience are natural postures, and thought is atrophied into the meaningless response of total conformity. This poses a rather serious problem.

For popular religion, as we understand and apply it, is inadequate for the needs of modern man in a space age. The effective level of religious revelation is but slightly removed, if at all, from primitive and outmoded concepts of man, earth and God.

Religion at its theoretical best, "pure and undefiled," is so rare in practice as to win for those who exemplify it the accolade of divinity, the confidence of supernatural implication — and often enough, the reward of "crucifixion." This is not to disparage religion unduly. Obviously a vast amount of good is done in its name. Yet it is difficult to escape the conclusion that, in a modern age, a machine as inefficient in the production of its major product as religion is of its major product, which might be said to be the good and full life for all, would either be rebuilt or scrapped.

In the effort to gain peace of mind and soul, maintain the status quo, enjoy the confidence of salvation and rationalize our failures, we remove from the realm of possible attainment in life the best in religion and the best in ourselves. Such a course is neither wise nor safe.

These are desperate times! In times of crisis, confusion, indecision, changing views and challenging problems, man hungers for certainty. In a sea of troubles, religion is an anchor to hold us firm and to keep us from drifting onto the shoals of secularism. But an anchor is designed to stop progress — and religion becomes obsolete if it stands still while everything else is changing. Moreover, man becomes irreligious in the act of resisting change and development.

But this hunger for certainty has been natural. To meet the demand, and perhaps to capitalize on it, there has been a rash of advice on how to secure peace, how to enjoy the benefits of positive thinking, and how to avoid frustration and doubt. To many, certainty and security seem to be guaranteed in the dogmatic asseverations so common in our religious culture. Today hardly anyone wants — or dares — to be "half-safe." And there is little reason to be if one can only accept the salvation that is offered for so little real effort on our part.

It would seem to make little difference that this security is, by and large, external and supernatural. Nor do we question the possibility that this positivism in the area of religion may be part of a rather fanatical effort to deny the existence of the spiritual inferiority complex from which we suffer. With so much positive emphasis on religion, it becomes unkind, may be considered disloyal and is rapidly becoming unpatriotic to question the validity or the efficacy of our beliefs. Anyone who so seeks publicly to evaluate cause and effect will not be popular. Clergymen, who should be at the forefront of religious progress, will be least able to speak out, for they too hunger — and hunger for certainty. They too have been indoctrinated with certain preconceptions, and they stand to suffer most from anything that might be considered heretical by superior, colleague or layman. This is not an insignificant point. For popular religion as we now enjoy it, is always based on emotion; and strongly religious people, so-called, have seldom been above persecution of those who disagree with them in their accepted and treasured beliefs. The true intellectual in the field of religion has been, if anything, even less popular than the intellectual or "egghead" in the field of politics. Faith has always been the substitute for intellectual scrutiny of basic theological premises. Faith may, indeed, be "the assurance of things hoped for, a conviction of things not seen" — but it is also a device by which primitive and outmoded concepts may be perpetuated to the detriment of the individual and society.

Today our religion depends more on faith than it ever did before. Protestant theologians have candidly asserted that the Christian gospel is a gift of grace beyond the limits of reason, that knowledge of God is beyond intellectual perception. Roman Catholic scholars are no less emphatic in this regard. It is as if "gospel truth," as we have learned it, can no longer be supported as truth save in a vacuum.

The trouble with faith, untutored by wisdom, is that it can make religion merely a conditioned reflex, perpetuating the old responses, uninfluenced by change and inadequately productive in a world that does change.

There is considerable evidence to indicate that the religious concern observable today — the so-called religious revival — may well be little more than conditioned reflex. As a matter of fact, this may account for much of our preoccupation with religion. We are conditioned by many things — among them heredity, environment, education, social and economic factors, personal desires, war and the threat of war. We are persuaded to go to church (which is somehow equated with being religious) by the hard and soft shell of professional pitchmen, well-meaning laymen and others who profit by popular "piousity." We find comfort and reassurance in the insertion of "under God" in our confirmation of allegiance. We print or stamp "In God We Trust" on our currency and the coin of the realm. But we do not trust in God, nor in the power of religion for good. We place a much greater trust in military might, which costs more, financially. And the State fosters belief in the efficacy of prayer by franking our postage with the admonition that we "Pray For Peace."

In the process, we seldom consider what God must be like. We seldom accept our personal responsibility to seek out and practice the things that make for peace. Nor do our religious leaders encourage the necessary soul-searching. Religion is designed to make the individual receptive to its truths rather than active in seeking out truth. The difference is the difference between instillation and distillation. Purity comes with the latter.

Be that as it may — whether this present preoccupation is "revival," "reversion" or "conditioned reflex" — we accept with rather disturbing complacency the idea that more religion or more religious indoctrination will somehow assure our salvation. It is almost as if we thought that, if we draw enough people into conformity with some "true faith," the sheer weight of numbers could bring God to intervene in world affairs on our behalf and settle the problems we have helped to create. To say the least, this is probably somewhat remote from the truth. It may even be dangerous illusion.

As a matter of fact, it may be worth considering that our problems take the form they do and are as great as they are, not because religion is lacking and needs to be re-emphasized, injected or superimposed, but more precisely because religion is actually being applied in accord with the level of revelation we have accepted. After all, we are products of our beliefs and no one (in Kahlil Gibran's words) "can separate his faith from his actions, or his belief from his occupations."

Yet it is important to note that "relations between men must continue so long as society continues, for it is these relations which constitute society. Therefore is society the problem of religion — and the new and ideal society its goal."[1] It thus seems eminently desirable that we examine religion objectively, as it affects our lives.

There are perhaps three possible ways of viewing the role of religion in society. We can believe that religion reached a point of perfect revelation some two thousand years ago, and that revelation was properly complete and sealed at that time. This idea prevails in our Christian culture despite certain modifications, evasions and mental reservations. In this view, man is sinful, inadequate, basically irresponsible and subject to salvation only by supernatural intervention. The positive power of religion which places a major emphasis — if not its major emphasis — on negative thinking about man is widely apparent, and makes a very real and dangerous impact on the individual and his society.

Man is inadequate in many ways. But whether he would be as inadequate as he now is, in regard to personal and social development, without religious reiteration of that inadequacy is an intriguing consideration. It would be a grave error to underestimate the significance of this fact. For we now know that man becomes neurotic when he fails to measure up to his potential. And man, in the aggregate as society, becomes "sick" when enlightened development is inhibited. Man has a psychological compulsion to live himself out. Religion, far from challenging that potential, has to a considerable extent smothered it. Man's energies have thus been diverted from the constructive fulfillment of the divine possibility inherent in every human life.

Organized religion itself, through the centuries, is largely responsible for the second view of the role of religion in society. Because rigidity, regimentation, segregation, selfishness, oppres-

---

(1) John Haynes Holmes, *Rethinking Religion*, New York, Macmillan, 1938, p. 81.

sion, persecution and worse have made their mark — often in excess of possible good — there has been, in some circles, a rejection of religion. Because religion has been inadequate, anti-religion (in the form of political Communism, for example) has become a tremendous force.

In any event, there has been a positive emphasis on man — his improvability, individually and collectively, and his ability to work out his own salvation without supernaturalism. If this has not always been evident, the opposition to religion as we know it has been apparent. Aversion for and the negative view of religion have led religious as well as secular groups to develop one or another type of humanism. In this group may be found some agnostics and atheists who, with little alternative, have abandoned God to the members of more orthodox groups who profess to know Him so well.

It is important to understand why these beliefs came into being. And it is a mistake too commonly made to group all these dissenters under one heading. Lest anyone consider this an indictment of humanism, it should be stated that humanism, at its best, may well have more validity as a truly religious expression than does theism as we know it. Yet, as there is a positive power in negative thinking about man, so there is a positive power in negative thinking about religion — and both are dangerous!

In the final analysis, no one rejects religion. Rejection seems evident only to those who feel that they alone have the "true faith" which others would deny. "Irreligion" is a label applied by the orthodox to those who refuse their Procrustean hospitality.

But traditional Christianity and humanism both, in their enlightened moments, approach a third and urgently needed explanation of the role of religion in society. This view holds that both man and religion are capable of improvement — that neither is yet complete or adequate and, by the very nature of things, cannot be. Those who hold this view frown on the suppression of religion by unenlightened negativism and political nihilism, on the one hand, and on the suppression of man and human potential by dogmatic and totalitarian religious forces, on the other. If we can accept the fact that both man and religion are improvable without supernatural intervention, we have the key to a vital, although not new, religious concept by which religion can continue to grow with new knowledge and man can be led forward to the limits of his potential.

If religion, as we know it and practice it, has been false to its trust, if we are threatened by antireligious forces, we need now to seek out "the more perfect way." Religion would seem to have no choice but to adjust to the fact of its inadequacy in the light of a broader yet grander view of man, his universe and his God.

I Am a Unitarian by Choice

by Mary Lou Page

I am a Unitarian by choice, not by conversion. By choice I jumped out of the circle of a traditional Christian religion into the wider circle of Unitarian philosophy, and I have been engaged in a continuous process of choosing ever since. This process of making choices has been a very significant part of my religion. In conversion, acceptance on faith almost automatically solves the many questions that surround this business of living and dying. But choosing the free or liberal religious way opened for me a life of choosing, of asking questions and trying to find answers: "Do I believe this?" and "Why?"

I got in this position because of a certain lack of choice in the orthodox church in which I was reared. This was a liberal Congregational church with an intelligent minister, but one who, it seemed to me, knew more about God than man can possibly know. The minister was very eloquent in talking to his congregation about God and about how God wanted us to act, and he was very convincing, as eloquence can be under certain circumstances. But to me there was a tremendous dichotomy between the church service and the real world I walked home in each Sunday. Where was the connection between this all-powerful spirit, this God of Love, this humble Jesus Christ, and the social hierarchy within the church, the quarreling people on street corners, the social and political ills which prevailed in the world? When I was troubled sufficiently, I summoned the courage to ask the minister about some of my doubts and about some of the contradictions which bothered me. He gave me the honest answer that I had to take the supernatural basis for his religion "on faith." I would find that if I believed his religion to be so, it would prove to be so; the answers would all work out in the end.

Well, I made my first significant choice right then. I did not choose to believe on faith, and so I started out on an honest but lonely road. I have often wondered why this kindly and intelligent man didn't tell me then that I had Unitarian leanings and that at least seventy-five thousand others in the United States took a similar position. As it was, I was alone — or almost alone, for I had been exposed to Ralph Waldo Emerson, and my youthful mind had already joyously reacted to such phrases as "Trust thyself: every heart vibrates to that iron string" and "It is easy in the world to live after the world's opinion; it is easy in solitude to live after our own; but the great man is he who in the midst of the crowd keeps with perfect sweetness the independence of solitude."

But as for my contemporaries, I was alone, or thought I was, in my way of thinking. It was actually eight years before I came across this phenomenon of Unitarianism, and nine years have passed since that time. During this period I have done a lot of reading, and I have taken a doubter's mind to most that I have read. This has been an exciting, if bewildering, time. It has been pretty much an experience of uphill struggles, and pauses on plateaus; of coming across new ideas and then giving them time to sink in and fit in with things as I saw them.

In one of his recorded sermons, "The Right to Disbelief," A. Powell Davies used the phrase "forging one's convictions" or "forging one's religion" as he recommended exposure to ideas and the independent use of one's mind. He added: "There is nothing to be feared from anything whatever that comes from anywhere at all into an honest mind. The one thing to fear is the mind's dishonesty." As I look back upon these years, it seems that my process of reading was one of exposing myself to as many ideas as I could be receptive to, and of forging my own religion out of them. In this process I have faced many ideas of which I have been fearful, but none has yet made me retreat for comfort to the orthodox position. Let me tell you some of these ideas.

First of all was the guilt that accompanies the act of rejecting the accepted religion of one's culture. There was the realization that this religion — Christianity, in my case — does work for some, and that many others who do not actually believe the religious dogmas manage to function in an established Christian church.

Then there was the question of the "place" of Jesus. To question the supernatural nature of his being is not enough. One must come to a positive position: What is the significance of this man? Is he more important than any other man who ever lived? Does he rank equally with the other great men — Socrates, Gandhi, Schweitzer?

The validity of religious experience other than the liberal was another problem to face. Are dogmatic religions just shams, all front with no content? Are people who take dogma as important being cheated out of the real essence of the religious concept? Or have they a "handle" on religion which merits respect and attention?

The next problem related to the audacity involved in striking out on one's own in the religious field. For one's resources are limited by one's intelligence, one's capacity to understand. I can understand just what I can understand, no more — and more intelligent people have already pursued this religious search and found answers. Why not accept their answers? Moreover, the state of physical and mental health affects one's capacity to reason, and there are times when one's own reasoning capacity is in question. Who is to know with certainty just when these times may be?

Then, of course, there was the problem of ethics. If one's system of ethics can't be said to come from God or the Bible or some other authoritative source, where does it come from? Society must behave itself — but on what basis?

Another problem which seemed very real to me was that of daring to live without an external structure or frame of reference. Sometimes I wondered, "Aren't you just kidding yourself in your strong moments? Perhaps when the chips are down you'll find all this is not an adequate philosophy or religion, but is just all words." I remembered from my high school days a poem called "The Hill" by Rupert Brooke, which ends:

    . . . . Proud we were
And laughed, that had such brave true things to say.
— And then you suddenly cried, and turned away.

Nor should I omit the practical problem of how to bring up my own children, when I myself was no longer sure what I thought about so many important things.

These are some of the problems that have confronted me, that have made me acutely uncomfortable at times and that I have been trying to resolve. I shall not try to answer them directly. Rather, I shall present some positive or constructive ideas which I have come to think significant and which impinge upon these problems. This is the most honest approach, for I make no pretense at this point of having formed a tight religious case.

In the first place, religion does not operate, as I had been taught to believe, in an area of fact. It is neither a science nor a suprascience. It is rather a psychological phenomenon, a need. Of course, the provable or truthful realities of the universe must "fit in" to one's religious scheme, but religion itself is not a system of provable facts and its resultant logic. To make a religion out of just what one knows is to take a dogmatic position, for one cannot fairly say that some condition he *doesn't* know — a soul, a spirit, an after-life — does not exist. The most one can say about it is that he doesn't know and isn't concerned with the problem. But neither is religion, as I had also been led to believe, an external truth which can be brought over and "fitted on" (through indoctrination), and thus assure one an ability to live life "right." For that is a dogmatic position too; it assumes a positive knowledge about unknowables as surely as denying such things assumes a knowledge.

Therefore my first point: religion is a psychological phenomenon, a need. A person emerges from childhood and suddenly stands back and looks at himself, and says, "Why, here am I — in this tremendous, overwhelming world. Why am I here? What is to become of me? Where do I fit in? What am I to do? How am I to act?" His answers to these questions constitute his religion.

A second idea that strikes me as sound is that Christianity is not the religion of Jesus: it is a religion about Jesus. If Jesus were to visit the Christian churches of today — if he observed the pageantry and stylized formulas in some, the emotional, revival-type behavior in others; and the well-ordered, conservative, aren't - we - doing - just - right - 11 - to - 12 - o'clock - Sunday - morning? attitude, in still others — I doubt that he would recognize his religion at all.

Erwin R. Goodenough, in *Toward a Mature Faith,* notes that men have projected many different images onto the historical figure of Jesus. Each new image gave men a new pattern with which they could align themselves, and he suggests that contemporary man can do the same. For although we know that this is the way mankind behaves, "we must not on that account cease to function! If we must function self-consciously, then let us have the courage to be self-conscious. This is one of the highest and rarest forms of courage. . . ."[1] and so he recommends that one read the New Testament and take from it what seems useful and sensible, with no regard to contradictions or context, and so formulate one's own faith, which he says will be in the direction of a mature faith. This led me to read the Bible again from a new approach.

A third — and equally perplexing — idea is one relating to man's values. Since I question the orthodox view of the universe, it is inevitable that I ask myself: Where do values come from? How do I know right and wrong?

Arnold Toynbee has said:

I believe we have no certain knowledge of what is right and wrong; and, even if we had, I believe we should find it just as hard as ever to do something that we knew for certain to be right in the teeth of our personal interests and inclinations. Actually, we have to make the best judgment we can about what is right, and then we have to bet on it by trying to make ourselves act on it, without being sure about it.[2]

---

(1) Erwin R. Goodenough, *Toward a Mature Faith,* New York, Prentice-Hall, Inc., 1955, p. 168.
(2) Arnold J. Toynbee, in *This I Believe,* Edward R. Murrow, ed., New York, Simon and Schuster, Inc., 1954, Vol. 2, p. 150.

Another person turned the apt phrase "All moral goods are human goods." And when I asked a Unitarian friend of mine where he got his values, he replied simply and easily, "I make them up." Well, I too think mankind makes them up and always has. I think the Ten Commandments were made up and presented to the Hebrew people in response to their need for a code of conduct at that time. I suppose one could turn the argument upside down, be more lyrical about it and say that, since Moses got his commandments from the finest thinking of his mind, he got them from God, and so that's where we get our values too. But this seems too poetic. I feel, quite simply, that man does form his own values and that this is a creative act and a statement of man's highest hopes.

The fourth concept I have come to recognize is the fact that some questions are unanswerable. It *is* possible to ask for more than mankind can answer, and one must learn to be comfortable with this uncomfortable fact. Of course, the real dilemma is that not everyone accepts this possibility. I am forever coming across articles and speeches telling with conviction things which, I realize in a more critical moment, are in the area of the unknowable. One remedy for this is to read nothing; a better solution is to read, or at least scan, many opinions. Whatever the case, I feel fairly adept now in separating the wish projections I read from the knowable ideas. And whenever I read articles proclaiming the unknowables, I am reminded of a couplet by Robert Frost:

> We dance round in a ring and suppose,
> But the Secret sits in the middle and knows.[3]

So on many questions I take an agnostic's position — that is to say, the position that I don't really know what's what. One of these questions is whether this is a planned or an unplanned universe; another is whether we are free agents or totally conditioned ceatures. I sometimes *act as though* one or the other of these is actually the case, for sometimes I feel I must take a

---

(3) "The Secret" in *Witness Tree*, New York, Henry Holt & Company, Inc.

position in order to be effective in my own life, even though I hold an agnostic view as to the truth of my position. (This reminds me of a statement by Schweitzer that it is wise to be both a "thorough-going rationalist and a thorough-going mystic.") I am always happy, however, when I find an authority who takes a point of view that I would like to hold, for the fact that some expert thinks my way gives the idea greater credence and makes me feel that at least I'm holding one of the accepted points of view of the intellectual world.

In short, I feel that there are many things we don't really know; yet we must act as though certain conditions do exist. And, of course, people are actually pushing back the frontiers of the unknowable all the time.

A fifth idea arises from the everyday world I live in as a wife and mother and friend — the fact that many people whose religion is of an orthodox nature find within their orthodox framework what I would call a valid religious experience. The many problems that made it impossible for me to hold to their position don't seem to bother them in the least. They have found in their religion the important things I have found in mine. We have the same concerns, the same desire for social action, the same ethics, even the same religious tolerance. Their religion is working for them to the same good end I hope mine is for me. Since these people are orthodox in their beliefs — God is real to them, and the divinity of Jesus is all important — it seems to me that there must be an area where all genuine religious experience can come together. There must be an area higher than — or deeper than — dogma or creed, where two souls can meet and understand each other.

I had a very interesting experience last year with a Missouri Synod Lutheran friend. I had been greatly excited by a play given by our local college in which I thought the humanist position was rather clearly spelled out. In this play, *Captive at Large,* the main character is looking for the "superintendent," the organizer of all things. He never finds him, but comes to the realization that man is his own superintendent. After the play, I asked my friend what she thought of it, expecting her to be dismayed. After all where was "God?" To my surprise, she thought the play was wonderful, and her pastor thought so too. "After all," she said, "the Lord does 'help those who help themselves,' and the effective Christian is one who realizes he must have the courage to make his own decisions and follow his own course." She from her framework and I from mine had both come to the same position — that we must have the courage to live our own lives as honestly and effectively as we can.

I therefore am compelled to be open to the idea that Christianity is "right" for some, and must be respected by me as such; and that I should at all times seek the level of mutual respect with my orthodox friends. I am reminded of a quotation from Mohammed:

Whatever be your religion, associate with men who think differently from you.
If you are a Muslim, go stay with the Franks.
If you are a Christian, mix with the Jews.
If you can mix with them freely and are not angered at hearing them,
You have attained peace and are master of creation.

I am grateful for the religious tolerance which is written into the laws of our lands, and I may some day come to a point of friction with my orthodox friends if my liberal religious freedom is threatened by political or legal means. In my personal relations, however, there seems to be no friction when I look deep. And on the surface it is often I who must remind myself to be tolerant and respectful of the other person's point of view.

The last major point I would like to make is that religion also encompasses the acceptance of ultimates — that is, coming to terms with the unknown or inevitable. This idea suddenly crystallized for me one day when I saw in a car one of those little Catholic statues of Christ with outstretched hands. Usually the sight annoys me a bit; but this time I suddenly realized that, for the believer, this statue was a symbol of being cared for, a symbol that everything would turn out all right. And this is a roundabout way of saying that what one must face, one can; it is an acceptance of the ultimate or the inevitable.

I thought then of the position of Socrates as reported in the *Crito:* "I see clearly that the time has arrived when it is better for me to die and be released from trouble. . . . Wherefore, be of good cheer about death, and know of a certainty, that no evil can happen to a good man, either in life or after death." I thought of the mystic, who finds peace because he feels "at one" with the universe. I was reminded also of a statement of the naturalist Donald Culross Peattie:

Yet the biologist, in confessing the mysterious ways of life, is not trying to create or maintain mysteries; he is not eager to be ignorant; he is not often a mystic, if that means a believer in the supernatural. For him the completely natural is strange enough. And great enough. And soul satisfying.

So, sometimes, he arrives at his own personal philosophy — a sense of being safe, safe in life. No one sees more keenly than he its cataclysms, its prodigious waste, the relentless operations of necessity. Life looks sometimes so terrible that he can find no peace save, like a gull, by resting on its waves, or, like the fawn, by sleeping in trust of the night and the things that in it are. In such trust one hardly expects special intervention, or any final quarter. The irreparable losses brought by death, the ultimate laying down of life itself, can be faced only through the courage that comes with the knowledge that mortal experience is shared.[4]

And I recalled a speech by a psychologist, Dr. James Bond, at the Midwest Unitarian Conference in which he said that people have different thresholds of anxiety, and that anxiety obstructs productiveness. "Ultimately," he said, "it's an either-or situation. Either you're an anxious personality, or you're a creative, constructive, productive personality." This made me suspect that the people who live creative, effective and construc-

---

(4) Donald Culross Peattie and Gordon Aymar, *This Is Living*, New York, Dodd, Mead & Company, 1938, Ch. 6.

tive lives are those who have come to accept the ultimates, the things they cannot know or change. Such people struggle, as we do, with problems in which they have a choice, in which decisions are possible. In fact, they have seen that man has more choices than may at first appear: he may question his mode of living and his cultural values, and he may balance his own actions between what society expects and what he himself wants out of life. But in the larger area of facing the inevitabilities and ultimates of life, such people have made their peace, their own synthesis. They no longer have that kind of anxiety which paralyzes man and obstructs creative work.

As for myself, I have not yet reached a real, deep synthesis of all the factors in a religious life, but I have found within Unitarianism a religious framework that seems valid. I can accept myself as I am — with my I.Q., my heritage, my conditioning, my aspirations — and say, "Here I stand, and this is how things look from here. I am doomed to meet sorrow, tragedy and death. But I take life on the terms that I received life. I was born with a capacity to grow and to feel and to know, and I shall use this capacity to its fullest. I shall think as deeply as I can. I shall feel the joy of living as deeply as I can. The tragedy and pain I will bear as well as I can; and I will try to build out of it, for I do not like pain. If, in coming to this point of view, I have aligned myself with some external realities, I am grateful; but if this is the all of life — so be it. It is worth all the effort it takes to live it."

But Find the Point Again

by Samuel H. Miller

When the climate of a culture changes, people are so preoccupied with their traditional habits and ways of looking at things that they do not see what is happening before their eyes. Revolutions come and go; states and empires fall; miracles rise from the ruins; yet they read their daily papers, eat and drink and sleep, suffer their sorrows, as if everything remained the same. They are supported by the structures of the past, to which they have been accustomed, and the new age rises unseen all about them. They are anachronisms, belonging to another age yet living in this one.

In religion the conserving tendency of faith exaggerates this indifference to the changing world. The church may long deceive itself by its spectacular success in numbers and prestige without knowing how hollow it has become,[1] or how feeble and unintelligible its message sounds to a world which has moved into new dimensions of knowledge and fear. The pulpit may continue to talk of matters long after their cogency has vanished, except in

---

(1) "Certainly by every test but that of influence the Church had never been stronger than it was at the opening of the twentieth century, and its strength increased steadily. Everyone was a Christian, and almost everyone joined some church, though few for reasons that would have earned them admission to Jonathan Edwards' Northampton congregation. The typical Protestant of the twentieth century inherited his religion as he did his politics, though rather more casually, and was quite unable to explain the differences between denominations. He found himself a church member by accident and persisted in his affiliation by habit; he greeted each recurring Sunday service with a sense of surprise and was persuaded that he conferred a benefit upon his rector and his community by participating in church services. The church was something to be 'supported' like some aged relative whose claim was vague but inescapable. . . .

"Never before had the church been materially more powerful or spiritually less effective."

Henry Steele Commager, *The American Mind,* New Haven, Yale University Press, 1950, pp. 166-67.

the sacred vocabulary of the preacher.[2] The ministry may be exhausted by the aggressive zeal of its diversified activities without touching the heart of darkness at the center of our troubled time.

Testy old Carlyle, in all his flamboyance, perceived this fact:

That a man stand there and speak of spiritual things to me, it is beautiful; even in its great obscurity and decadence it is among the beautifulest, most touching objects one sees on this earth. This speaking man has indeed, in these times, wandered terribly from the point; has, alas, as it were, totally lost sight of the point, yet at bottom whom have we to compare with him? Of all such functionaries boarded and lodged on the industry of modern Europe, is there one worthier of the board he has? . . . The speaking function, with all our writing and printing function, has a perennial place, could he but find the point again![3]

Worthy of his bed and board — if he could but find the point again! Age after age he had served well. According to the needs of previous epochs, he had stood in the teeth of the storm; despite unpopularity and even martyrdom, he had not wavered from the point nor betrayed the nature of his leadership. Think only of the apostles, who had fashioned the profound bases of Christian civilization, sustaining for centuries the life and culture of many peoples; or of the priests who had labored in many fields, in the arts and in philosophy, during the Middle Ages, elaborating a world which reached its climax in cathedral and *summa;* or of the reformers who had endured the ordeal of a radical revolution in the ways of faith and modes of action, transforming the institutions of the state and church in terms of new freedoms. Where did Carlyle's speaking man lose the

---

(2) "The great biblical key ideas of sovereign divine creation, election, sin, mercy, judgment, conversion, rebirth, reconciliation, justification, sanctification, Kingdom of God, are utterly alien, and consequently irrelevant to people whose minds are molded and dominated by the conquest of the kingdom of man. They are undecipherable hieroglyphs, with which, strangely enough, Church people still seem to play." Hendrik Kraemer, *The Communication of the Christian Faith,* Philadelphia, Westminster Press, 1956, p. 94.

(3) Thomas Carlyle, *Past and Present,* Bk. IV, Chap. 1, "Collected Works," Vol. VII, London, 1870.

point? Was he meandering, fiddling at inconsequentials? Was
he blind, or stupid, or wicked? A world was in the making, as
every epoch makes its world, and this man did not keep to his
job. He strayed, and in his straying the bonds of faith were
loosed, and the world fell apart.

Now you and I are standing in that man's shoes. We too
have been called to minister to the world. Will we have anything
to say, not merely to please the world, but to fit its real needs?
Will we able to find the point again and thus provide a firm base
for society, perspectives sufficient for the arts and culture, and an
intellectual integrity profound enough to discipline the destructive forces of our present chaos?

Our fundamental embarrassment as we stand face to face
with this world is that we may become relevant to its demands
all too easily, conforming to that standard which the world sets
for us, and so lose the very point of being a minister in the
world. One of the tragedies of our time is that the minister is
both overworked and unemployed: overworked in a multitude of
tasks that have not the slightest connection with religion, and
unemployed in the serious concerns and exacting labors of maintaining a disciplined spiritual life among mature men and
women. It is a scandal of modern Protestantism that young men
called to the high venture of the Christian way, disciplined by
seminary training in the arduous dimensions of such faith, are
graduated into churches where the magnitude of their vocation
is as Joseph Sittler has said, *macerated,* chopped into small pieces
by the pressure of the petty practices of so-called parish progress.
One wonders how much of the compulsive frenzy of the parish
minister comes from the guilty realization that he has not attended to his prime calling, but is merely filling up time with a
nervous pandemonium of jerks and jabs toward people in order
to make the church popular. Wherever the current ideal of the
minister comes from — the big operator, the smart salesman, the
successful tycoon — it still remains a puzzle why the minister
should fall prey to such false images, unless he has completely
confused what he is supposed to be doing with what most
churches want him to do.

Herman Melville, as flamboyant a rhetorician as Carlyle, yet with profound perceptions of the minister's task, described the pulpit in the New Bedford Whalemen's Chapel where the one-time harpooner, Father Mapple, preached.

The pulpit is ever this earth's foremost part. All the rest comes in its rear; the pulpit leads the world. From thence it is the storm of God's quick wrath is first described, and the bow must bear the earliest brunt. From thence it is that the God of breezes fair or foul is first invoked for favorable winds. Yes, the world's a ship on its passage out, and not a voyage complete; and the pulpit is its prow.[4]

This might easily have been accepted at face value in the early nineteenth century, but for us it would be easier to believe it was written tongue in cheek, a rather fatuous inflation of words and little more. The truth is that the pulpit, at least now, is certainly *not* the prow of this world, dividing new seas with its bold bow. The pulpit does not lead the world, either in generating power or in initiating ideas. It is set back now in quieter waters, out of the haste and the traffic, where strife is real and decisions must be made.

The world is still a ship on its passage out. There is no doubt of that, nor that the voyage is incomplete. Indeed, we are more uncertain than Melville as to where we are going. Our charts seem obsolete in the light of new facts and forces; we approach the unknown with a dread as terrifying as that the first man must have felt when he ventured out of sight of land under strange skies. The minister, no less than others, has been overwhelmed by the catastrophic changes of history.

If the ministry is to regain its magnitude and integrity, it must be validated at a much more serious level of life than that of success and prestige. To succumb either to sentimental popularity or to institutional professionalism is to betray both our own calling and the world's need. The ministry has a point, a tip of light which breaks the darkness like a sharpened spear — a bright moment when the diversity and contradictions of life

---

(4) Herman Melville, *Moby Dick*, Boston, Houghton Mifflin Co., 1956, p. 50.

break into a unity, never complete and never permanent, but always redemptive and profoundly satisfying. We prove ourselves at the point where we enter into history, where the world is being made and unmade, where life turns into hell or opens into heaven; where, like Jacob of old, men and women are caught in the middle of the darkness, alone and in agony, wrestling with the unnamed mysteries of existence, striving to exact a blessing from the exigencies of their human lot. We come to life as a profession when we stand forth, beyond the superficial safety and the limits of praise and blame, to speak the clumsy, daring word that only faith may speak — of things unseen but powerful with portent to be; of realities waiting to be born at the far edge of all things known; of a realm mysterious with blessing for any who can become like little children, able to leap beyond themselves to a greatness dimly surmised.

Yet any man who steps into this kind of pulpit, into this prow where the storms strike first and the dark is thickest, knows well the terror of his position. The ministry in any age is caught between the offense of God and the offense of the world: between the awful terror of making God plain, of speaking the *verbum dei,* and the terrifying muddle of this world's jumble of circumstances, in which human life is crucified. Like a lonely figure, the ministry in our age stands separated both from the confident assurance of any infallible, or perhaps even divine, message easily inherited from the past, and from the arrogance of an age which finds all authority in itself. We may stand at the prow, but not with the sustaining authority our forefathers found in their Bibles, their creeds and their churches; and the seething waters that break across our bow are from deeper seas than any man has ever sailed. As J. Robert Oppenheimer has said:

> This is a world in which each of us, knowing his limitations, knowing the evils of superficiality and the terrors of fatigue, will have to cling to what is close to him, to what he knows, to what he can do, to his friends and his tradition and his love, lest he be dissolved in a universal confusion and know nothing and love nothing. . . .

This balance, this perpetual, precarious, impossible balance between the infinitely open and the intimate, this time — our twentieth century — has been long in coming; but it has come. It is, I think, for us and our children, our only way. . . . This cannot be an easy life. We shall have a rugged time of it to keep our minds open and to keep them deep. . . .[5]

Only the utmost honesty, perhaps the confession of our poverty, will enable us in this extremity to prove ourselves a skilled profession worthy of its bed and board.

To say the least, our situation is bewildering. T. S. Eliot commented that much of our heritage is Christian, but vastly less so than it used to be. The whole imaginative structure of Christian truth, elaborated in myth and symbol, has for the most part crumbled under the impact of the last three centuries of revolutionary thought, scientific methods and historical studies. The vision of reality articulated in this great biblical formulary has evaporated and no longer serves as the frame of reference for elucidating the mysteries of being human. We have not deliberately renounced our Christian heritage, but it no longer plays a dynamic role in motivating our actions or in guiding us as we evaluate our satisfactions. Men are no longer moved by the words which once thrust men to war or turned them from the world to God. The charts which men have used for centuries seem quite inadequate in the face of new conditions. The character of reality for human beings has changed, and the ancient vision is no longer sufficient.

Shall we, then, labor to create a new Christian culture with materials coming from the new discoveries, disciplines and attitudes of our time; or shall we succumb to an essentially nonreligious — that is, a subpagan — culture?[6] It has always been the function of faith to supply a structure of myth and symbol,

---

(5) J. Robert Oppenheimer, *Man's Right to Knowledge*, 2nd. Series, New York, Columbia University Press, 1955, p. 115.

(6) "The civilization characteristic of Christendom has not disappeared, yet another civilization has begun to take its place . . . Our whole life and mind is saturated with the slow upward filtration of a new spirit — that of an emancipated atheistic international democracy." George Santayana, *Winds of Doctrine*, New York, Harper & Bros., 1957, p. 1.

and to enact in appropriate rites a vision of reality capable of
sustaining the larger inferences of meaning in the life of a people
— a vision which provides for the exercise of freedom in human
possibilities, but which is not reducible to precise, black-and-
white, static literalisms.[7] It is such a symbolic structure of the
imagination which ties together the disparate realities and forces
of human existence, and at the same time becomes a vocabulary
(verbal, visual and active) by which a community can be established and, under certain conditions, can rise to the level of
communion. Wherever this symbolic structure evaporates, loses
its power of suggestion, becomes dogmatically rigid and then
superficially literal, the people lose their means of coherence.
The ancient dictum is still true: where there is no vision of commonly recognized reality, the people perish as a people, society
falls apart, and civilization and culture are thrown into anarchy
and self-destruction. Lewis Mumford, in his Bampton Lectures,
declared:

> Perhaps the fatal course all civilizations have so far followed
> has been due, not to natural miscarriages, the disastrous effects of
> famines and floods and diseases, but to accumulated perversions
> of the symbolic functions.[8]

Our disorders, I suspect, derive from the fact that the vision
of reality conceived in redemptive terms and elaborated by Dante
and Aquinas is simply no longer suggestive for multitudes conditioned by the popular influences of science and industry. The
minister, if he is to be useful to the rehabilitation of society and
the redemption of the individual, cannot offer the twentieth century the image which the thirteenth century found eminently
satisfactory. The new age has a style of its own, a language
peculiar to itself; and whatever image of reality is to be conjured
up must be of the very substance of our time. On the other hand,

---

(7) "The great social ideal for religion is that it should be the common
   basis for the unity of civilization . . . In that way it justifies its insight
   beyond the transient clash of brute force." Alfred North Whitehead,
   Adventures of Ideas, New York, The Macmillan Co., 1933, p. 221.
(8) Lewis Mumford, *Art. Technics,* New York, Columbia University Press,
   1952, p. 51.

the minister can scarcely believe that the twentieth century, unlike all others, has transcended the limitations of time and history so that it is sufficient to itself.[9] A vision of reality limited only to our own epoch is incredibly arrogant and stupidly parochial. The golden-tongued Chrysostom put it well, as he put many things: "A priest must be sober and clear-eyed, with a thousand eyes in every direction."

New configurations of experience have arisen in the Renaissance, the Industrial Revolution and the rise of science, each with its own system of values and perspectives of discrimination by which life is ordered. We have moved out of the Magical Age, as I. A. Richards has put it, into the Scientific. We have reached a new maturity of freedom from superstition and credulity. With this *Mündigkeit,* or adulthood, as Bonhoeffer describes it, there has occurred an extraordinary activity and excitement in all the creative aspects of man's mind and spirit. New life is erupting in fresh but ambiguous forms which need identification and judgment. To evaluate such a burgeoning mass of new work is not easy, but it is evident that much of it approximates or reflects the ancient and traditional expressions of religious concerns about the elemental mysteries of human existence.

Into the vacuum left by the slow evaporation of the biblical image of reality, the burgeoning powers of this age have understandably and desperately pushed their way, seeking to formulate a new and more congenial vision of reality. The arts have gone philosophical. Beckman, Klee, Picasso, Henry Moore deliver their gnomic elucidations about the nature of reality with religious seriousness. The sciences too, finding themselves on the brink of this same vacuum, have not always been slow to make a leap of faith concerning ultimate things; and when the scientists themselves have modestly desisted, their friends have rushed in with cosmic conclusions. Even business, for all its pragmatic

---

(9) "Any modern re-formation of the religion (based upon certain historical occasions scattered irregularly within a period of about 1200 years from the earlier Hebrew prophets to the stabilization of theology by Augustine) must first concentrate upon the moral and metaphysical intuitions scattered throughout the whole epoch." Whitehead, *op. cit.,* p. 212.

traditions and prejudices, has become quite confidently responsible and evangelical, urging upon men and their families the "business way of life."

The minister must confront these twin terrors of the pulpit — at his back what seems to be an obsolete order of things and before him a confusion from which nothing is exempt. He stands for a whole congeries of notions which have become mere words, and he must deal with a turbulent age doing its best to create a new order of intelligible meaning. Now that the Christian vision no longer reverberates in the life of man, how will the minister find the insight or the courage to proclaim "good news"? How will he rehabilitate the heights and depths of sensibility which have atrophied in the recent frenzy of naturalizing the world? How will he demonstrate the reality of life at levels from which man has long since withdrawn to busy himself in other areas? How will he speak to the point when man has nothing in his experience to help him perceive such realities as grace and spirit?

Can the minister supply a vision of reality? Can he offer the Bible to a people disabused of its validity? Can he recall heaven and hell to a people who have laughed them out of existence? Can he talk to them of God, when they find God quite unimaginable in a world scientifically structured in iron law? Can he explain faith, redemption, grace, while they think rather of the defense mechanisms of the ego and the libidinous expressions of the id? Can he continue to conduct the rites of the church and speak of "holy" things, when life itself has been naturalized and even the church measures its own significance by statistical categories and popular prestige?

Sharing in this demythologized epoch, he may have no vision of reality to offer. But if there is no vision, there is no preacher, no message, no church. He cannot peddle Dante or Thomas, Luther or Calvin, as if nothing had happened in the world since their time. As Kierkegaard so succinctly put it, one cannot crib the answers to the problems of the age from the back of the book.

If ever the conditions of the world demanded the highest and most rigorous intellectual preparation for the ministry, they do so now. The founders of Harvard University were profoundly convinced that no well-ordered society could long endure without a "learned ministry." Well into the eighteenth century this passionate conviction was expressed, until the twin forces of pietism and romanticism began to dull the edge of all discipline in American life. Slackness, emotionalism and a fever of optimism spread through the church and corrupted its ways. There was a general levelling of all classes in the name of democracy, and a revolt against all theological thoroughness in the name of simplicity and practical concerns. By and large, there was a loose vulgarization of the Christian faith, which by the early twentieth century had transformed it into a shadow of the moral enthusiasms and respectability of the secular world. We must again reassert the fundamental necessity for a learned ministry, if the church is to survive as a potent source of that vision by which society unites its life in a meaningful order of truth and goodness. The church's present tactics are scarcely more than an effort to keep its body alive by repudiating its soul.

Only by dint of the severest intellectual discipline can a man provide a vision of reality for such an age as this. If that vision is in the Christian tradition, he must discover how to unwrap it, reveal its dynamic suggestiveness, make plain its elucidation of the human problem. If it is not in the Christian tradition, he must discover where it is and what it is. In either case, he must be able to make wise and revealing judgments, not confusing truth with novelty, nor tradition with truth, but distinguishing between appearance and reality, between the authentic and the popular. To be wise about the living past in the present, to confirm the eternal in the temporal and to discriminate sharply between sophisticated skepticism and skeptical faith — this is an order of considerable magnitude. It is certainly no job for an ecclesiastical mechanic or a general manager of parish programs. The radical thrust of this work is in the direction of the most profound perceptiveness, imagination, rational daring and penetrating insight.

As in other professions, and nowhere more disastrously, American practicality has contrived short cuts in the training of the ministry. Concerned only with shortsighted results, it has reduced theological education to a vulgarized form of a trade school, where facile schemes, glib formulas and manipulative methods prepare a man for disillusionment and heartsickening bitterness, when he discovers all too late that such bright and shining stones are no food for the hunger of honest men and women, touched by this world's tragic pain. If there is to be a vision of reality, if the minister really desires to find the point again and be worthy of his board, he can do so only by probing the Bible to its deepest ground, exploring the wide reaches of faith in its historical elaboration and articulating, as explicitly as his imagination and reason allow, the theological structure of human relationships and circumstantial mysteries. Certainly no portion of his intellectual ability can be left undeveloped.

A great deal of nonsense, especially in pietistic circles (and supported by a native American anti-intellectualism), has been uttered in this regard. The attainment of the saints has been praised as if they achieved it either without or in spite of intelligence. Neither history nor biography corroborates such an illusion. A soft-headed saint is simply no saint. Although the saints may not have been scholars, their intelligence was undeniable. One can scarcely fulfill the love of God in Jesus' prime commandment without the passionate expression of the "whole mind." Let the minister be sure his mind is sharpened to its utmost, lest he blunder about the world with a rough and stupid carelessness, hoping that he might hit upon the will of God merely because of his good intentions.

The minister has a job of monumental dimensions. The specifications for rehabilitating a usable, imaginable, worshipful vision of reality in our time are such as to thrust a man beyond all the normal limits of his resources. He must search the past till he finds the quick of it — and knows beyond doubt the broad and everlasting realities in it which run like a living stream into our own day. He must probe the present, suffer the full brunt of its tumultuous power and passion, and separate with painful threshing the wheat from the chaff in his own mind and heart. He must take the Bible, a very old book fashioned in archaic languages and forms, and unveil the present intimacy of its radical realities. He must handle the perplexing chaos of mortal circumstance, the old and the new, the great and the inconsequential, the sacred and the profane; and by an alchemy of his own he must make sense of things, or be honest and humble in knowing that he can do no more than face them wisely and bravely. He must learn to see the primordial truth in small events, the sublime in common, unexpected places, the glory of grace in humble persons, the son of God in a "litter of scorn." Everywhere he must have eyes to see what mortal eyes too often miss, and the intelligence both to look for it and to confirm it when it is found.

André Malraux, the novelist, has one of his characters ask, "How can one make the best of one's life?" Another answers, "By converting as wide a range of experience into conscious thought as possible." This is, in a sense, the function of the minister, especially if we keep in mind the tremendous scope of "experience" and the dialectical forces of history producing it. The intelligence of the minister is redemptive: he not only turns experience into conscious thought, but seeks to make sense out of the diversity and incompleteness of experience. His task is to bring experience to conscious fulfillment, and to articulate that fulfillment in terms of an ultimate whole. The vision of reality is seen in small events and single revelations; it becomes the symbol of the total way of life in which all things work together for good to them that love God. He will sadly know how true it is that, as Proust once said, most lives are like camera film, exposed to passing events but never developed. It is the joy and anguish of the minister to "develop" the experience of men to a vision of reality.

Some words of Albert Camus, spoken when he received the Nobel Prize, are a thrust of light in this direction. Although he spoke of art, his thoughts apply equally well to religion:

> To me art is not a solitary delight. It is a means of stirring the greatest number of men with a privileged image of our common joys and sorrows. Hence it forces the artist [minister] not to

isolate himself; it subjects him to the humblest and most universal truth.

Not one of us is great enough for such a vocation. . . . Whatever our personal frailties may be, the nobility of our calling will always be rooted in two commitments difficult to observe: refusal to lie about what we know and resistance to oppression.

Faced with a world threatened by disintegration, in which our grand inquisitors may set up once and for all the kingdoms of death, this generation knows that, in a sort of mad race against time, it ought to reestablish among nations a peace not based on slavery, to reconcile labor and culture again, and to reconstruct with all men an Ark of the Covenant.[10]

"To reconstruct with all men an Ark of the Covenant"! To bind together in one household the humanity of our time; to recover the ground of truth on which we all must stand, and the vision of hope in which freedom may be boldly exercised; to lift up our eyes to that higher dream of which Dante spoke, in which the exuberance of our epoch may become, not a haunted nightmare or a burden of despair, but a song of joy and peace for all people. This is a calling beyond our strength, yet nothing less could demand or deserve our all. It is Dante again who emblazons the text for such a calling in his unforgettable words, "I crown and mitre thee above thyself." Not in our strength, not in our wisdom, but in the power of that which waits to be born, in the new Ark of the Covenant, we stake our faith.

To train men for such a profession has never been an easy task. In our day an educated man may pass as such by having a wide smattering of slight contacts, innumerable opinions and a name-dropping vocabulary. Sometimes theological education has contented itself with informing men with more than they can think, and encouraging a kind of lust for knowledge which accumulates a body of inert ideas in lieu of wisdom. If we can keep in mind that Ark of the Covenant for which Camus is striving, out of motives far removed from the Christian faith,

---

(10) Albert Camus, quoted by Charles Rolo, "Albert Camus: A Good Man," *The Atlantic Monthly*, Vol. 201, No. 5, May 1958.

we too will know that there is something greater than our particular art or our special skill. The fragmentation of the world is mirrored in our divisive authorities. Our vocabularies tend to become departmental or even private. The paths of communication and of possible unity become clogged with protective devices and defensive barriers for our private satisfactions. The walls which separate so much of our learning in seemingly watertight compartments are not in life. We make them ourselves, sometimes for our convenience, often for our prestige; but we must find a way to breach them if we are to train men to love God with their whole mind.[11]

A learned ministry is not necessarily pedantic. Indeed, a minister is in many respects a disciplined amateur. He is amateur because he works forever at the edge of unprecedented possibilities in the freedom by which the spirit fulfills events and needs. He is amateur because he is concerned with everything human, across the entire spectrum of sensibility from feeling to idea to action. He is amateur because he is a lover of this world, intent on fulfilling its deepest and most radical reality through its diversified institutions and cultures. As an amateur, he will want to draw together insight and perception from every corner of time and space. He will meditate, day and night, on those primordial myths in which the experience of multitudes was strained, concentrated and objectified in archaic figures and forms. He will read the long and troubled contours of the past, the profound penetrations of prophet and priest, the dreams and corruption and heroism of the church, the anguish of centuries and the hope of eternity. To know; to know accurately and deeply; to respect the fullness of our inheritance; to study it with earnest discipline; to explore it humbly and expectantly for its peculiar gift to the wisdom of the ages; and to discover in it the

---

(11) "The doctor, the teacher, the administrator, the judge, the clergyman, the architect are each in his own way professionally concerned with man as a whole, and the conditions of human life as a whole. Preparation for these professions is unthinking and inhuman if it fails to relate us to the whole." Karl Jaspers, *The Idea of the University*, Boston, Beacon Press, 1959, p. 47.

opening of the deeper levels of present existence — this requires intelligence of the most disciplined sort, but not pedantry.

Every profession of our time increasingly demands a skill of theoretical knowledge and practical application; and the ministry, no less than any other, must be a disciplined profession. By and large, we are not so at present. We have bartered our professional birthright of an honored place in the economy of a community by reducing our office to a mad dervish dance of unenlightened public activities. Our duty is still intellectual in the highest sense of that term.

I will not say that you cannot be ordained as a minister without some vision of reality by which human experience can be elucidated, its heights and depths articulated, and its risk of waste redeemed for meaning and joy. I will not say you cannot serve the church in many different ways without such a standard of measurement and discernment. I will not say that you cannot help people in many of their crises when the spirit despairs and life grows dark. But I *will* say that if you enter the ministry and hope to stand in the pulpit as the prow of the world, in the foremost part where directions are discerned and determined; if you expect to serve the real needs and not merely the apparent needs of the time in which you live; if you are going to find the point again where the ministry can be validated as a profession competently intent on doing its own job — in short, if you hope to minister truly to men — you must find a way to pull life together, in a frame of reference or in a vision of reality, so that men will know the dignity of belonging to this vast venture under God. Only by stretching ourselves to the utmost, by submitting both to the discipline of training and to the conditions of the time in which we work, will we prepare ourselves to make meaning out of the cataclysms of history or the humble events of human experience. Until we find the point again and stand by it boldly, intelligently, the pulpit will be no more than an easy refuge from the strife and pain of life. But if we find the point again, if the vision is restored and the word is spoken for which every age waits, then no man will claim our place.

"Will Ye Speak Falsely for God?"

by Frank M. Cross, Jr.

Here is a summary of the book of Job, designed for use in churches and Sunday schools: "The author of the dialogues of Job tells of the patience of a pious man during a siege of boils. He explains how God may bring evil upon an innocent man as a means to test and thereby deepen his faith. Job maintains his faith in the righteousness of God throughout his ordeal. Although he speaks overboldly at times, he also gives voice to memorable affirmations of faith: 'Though he slay me, yet will I trust in him' and 'I know that my Redeemer liveth. . . .' In short, the poet declares that the just man who perseveres will be blessed in life — and if not in life, at least in a world to come."

Each statement I have read thus far about Job is false. Indeed, this was my malicious intent in composing the quotation. But in thus caricaturing the dialogues of Job, I am in Christian company. I suspect that I have not distorted unfairly the version of Job expounded from the American pulpit. The book of Job is probably the most grotesquely mistreated book in the Bible, although there has been a brisk competition for this honor.

The Job of the dialogues is not a patient man. He is an angry man, an honest man, a despairing man, but not a patient man. Again, Job's complaint was not primarily physical in origin. To be sure, he was suffering from this world's most vexatious torments — a skin disease and a nagging wife. In the dialogues, however, his physical distress is only the occasion for his suffering, not its ground. His weariness is the weariness of despair, and his fever is inflamed by the heat of his wrath against implacable heaven. He cries out against the anxiety and meaninglessness of human life lived under the shadow of death: "Man is a wretched creature bound up in dust and short days." In modern terms, Job is saying that man is cruelly imprisoned in his mortality, chained in the hateful finiteness of flesh.

From this weak, dying creature, God has required eternal

loyalty. He has imposed upon him the responsibility proper to freedom and knowledge, yet man finds his freedom qualified, his knowledge darkened. When his loyalty fails, however, he is "pursued like a leaf before the wind" by an angry God who searches out his sin. As Job protested:

Am I Yamm [the dragon of chaos], the [primordial] monster
That thou dost mount guard over me? . . .
Leave me alone, for my days are as a breath.
What is man that thou dost make so much of him?
That thou dost set thy mind on him,
Dost visit him every morning and test him every moment?
Why dost thou not turn thy gaze from me,
Or let me relax until I swallow my spittle?
If I have sinned, then what have I done to thee,
O thou watcher of men?
Why dost thou make me thy target?
Am I become such a burden to thee?
Why not simply forgive my transgression
Or ignore my guilt?
A moment and I shall lie in the dust;
Thou shalt look about for me, and I shall not exist.

[Job 7:12, 16b-21]

Job is the archetype of K in Kafka's *The Trial,* condemned by a remorseless justice and burdened by an awful guilt for an unknown or forgotten crime. His words describe the world which lies under the curse of a hidden God — or, if you choose, the world which has murdered its God. His is a world we all know secretly, but which we have joined in an unconscious conspiracy to ignore, at least in church. Job's anger is the gauge of his revulsion against the meaninglessness of life-unto-death — or more precisely, the plight of mortal but guilty humanity.

Again, Job's dialogues provide no explanation of innocent suffering. The prologue, to be sure, contains at least an implicit answer: it interprets the suffering of the righteous by telling of God's decision to test Job. But this is the very barrier to the understanding of Job which has blocked accurate exegesis for more than two thousand years and which has been removed only by modern historical study. The author of the dialogues bor-

rowed from a popular and traditional folk tale the characters
and the setting for his dialogues. The old tale was recounted in
a prologue and epilogue, either by the author himself or by the
traditionists who preserved his work. Although the dialogues
depend at many points on the background furnished by the tale,
their bitter, poetic polemic against conventional piety cannot be
harmonized with the simple, inoffensive folk story. Ironically, in
the history of the interpretation of Job, the dramatic little tale
has often overpowered the rhetorical force of the dialogues and
proved more satisfying to the godly. The tale is neatly con-
structed: the Lord slaughters the seven sons and three daughters
of Job and, when they are killed, arranges for Job to beget seven
sons and three daughters more. This is perfect justice . . . numerically. Who could complain — except, perhaps, Job's weary
wife?

The dialogues of Job do *not* celebrate Job's steadfast faith
in the righteous rule of God. His apparent affirmations of faith
require scrutiny. A favorite text from the Authorized Version,
"Though he slay me, yet will I trust in him," reads in the earliest
form of the text: "Behold he will slay me. I have no hope." The
reference to a living redeemer alludes neither to a pre-existent
Son of Man nor to a future salvation. It is a mythological reference to an angelic advocate in the heavenly court, an advocate
who will declare Job's integrity for the official record, presumably
after his death. Far from asserting his faith, Job is seeking to
force his three friends, who are defending God with religious
platitudes, to recognize that the human community is characterized by rampant, ubiquitous injustice.

The dialogues themselves attack the unifying tent of Israel's
contemporary faith — "the godly shall inherit the earth." Israel's
faith was bound in an historical frame. God was the God of gods
who delivered his people from Egypt. The fathers in the faith
saw their escape from the prison house of Goshen, not as the
capricious act of an unknown god, but as the definitive act of
their God, now revealed as the God Who delivers men from a
slavery which is death-in-life to a freedom which is authentic life.
Israel's God was He Who revealed the destiny of Israel — and

mankind's destiny — in the overthrow of human tyrannies and lordships, and in the creation of a community whose sole lord was God Himself. He was now seen as the God who blessed the weak and poor, and chose for Himself the imprisoned and dying. He disclosed his power and freedom in human history to establish his elect in a community of peace.

In the national development of Israel's religion, the confessions of this historical faith were elaborated. The Lord of Israel, it was said, will deliver an obedient nation, and He will bring down by plague or defeat a rebellious and proud people. Israel's school of pious and wise men further simplified and refined the older doctrines. The ancient Lord of Israel's community became the God of the pious individual; He prospered the godly in his lifetime and struck down the unrighteous in the midst of his folly. Thus weal and woe were the unambiguous signs of God's pleasure or wrath, direct evidence of man's integrity or sin.

The author of the dialogues proposed to refute this orthodox doctrine of the Divine economy. The scope of his debate is limited. In appropriating the legend of Job, he avoids using the stock biblical hero, the wretch who has sinned boldly; thereby he simplifies the issues and prejudices his reader's verdict. In his attack on the orthodox doctrine of history, there is no hint of what may be called the communal and eschatological categories in which Israel's faith was classically cast. The Job of the dialogues is an isolated man, whereas it is the community which provides the normal biblical context of salvation. There is no expected fulfillment in a new historical or transhistorical era, giving significance to the life of the community and hence to the person in the community. There is no "external" dimension of the historical flow of human existence. Job's history is the span of his days. He and his comforters scan this limited history, their age, their old heaven and earth, for signs of grace or a just providence.

Eliphaz sets out the orthodox thesis, echoed and elaborated through the dialogues by his fellow defenders of the faith:

Think now, who that was innocent ever perished, or where were
    the righteous destroyed?

As I have observed, those who plow falsehood and sow trouble
reap the same;
By the breath of God they perish, and by the blast of his wrath
they are consumed.

[Job 4:7-9]

[God] sets on high the lowly, and the despondent are lifted in
victory.
He frustrates the designs of the crafty, so that their hands achieve
no success. . . .
[He delivers the orphan from violence (?)], the poor from the
hand of the strong.
So the pauper has hope, and injustice shuts her mouth.

[Job 5:11, 12, 15, 16]

Job describes the actual world he knows:

Look at me, and be appalled, and put your hand on [your]
mouth.
When I call it to mind, I shudder, and chills seize my flesh.
Why do the wicked live, reach old age — yea, and wax great in
power?
Their children are established before them, and their progeny be-
fore their eyes.
Their houses are free from anxiety, and God's rod [falls] not on
them. . . .
They spend their days in prosperity, and in peace go down to
Sheol. . . .
When you say, "Where is the house of the prince?" "Where is
the camp of the wicked?"
Have you not asked those who travel the roads, and do you not
accept their evidence:
That the wicked man is spared in the day of calamity, that he is
rescued in the day of wrath?

[Job 21:5-9, 13, 28-30]

The cycles of the dialogues go round. Job listens impatiently and replies impatiently to the eloquent apologetics of his
three friends. He suffers restlessly their pastoral tones, their
pious pomposity, their offense at his doubts, their refusal to admit
questions and their endless stock of brilliant aphorisms. He observes that they are liars:

Will you tell lies in God's behalf and speak falsely for him?
Will you show him partiality; will you prejudge the case in his
    favor?
Will it go well when he examines you? Can you delude him as
    you delude a man?
Nay, he will surely punish you if you secretly show him partiality.

[Job 13:7-10]

These words are not inappropriate as a salutation to young
men and women entering a Protestant divinity school, or to
teachers and scholars engaging in theological conversation, or to
ministers propagating the biblical faith. The church, through
its ministers, scholars and apologists, speaks falsely for God. We
speak falsely through simple ignorance. More frequently, we
lie in *guilty* ignorance, confusing the word of the church with the
Word of God, identifying the claims of the human institution of
the church with those of the invisible Body of Christ. And sometimes we lie with cold premeditation to promote our product and
our institution.

Witness the conventional dishonesty which grips the Christian pulpit. In the tradition of the Reformation, the pulpit
performs a single, central function: here the Bible is to be laid
open and the biblical faith expounded. The form of this tradition
is preserved in the modern church, but our preaching little re-
sembles biblical exposition. For one thing, few clergymen can
read the Bible in its original languages; they depend on secondary
sources, translations and commentaries. No doubt the latter have
their uses. But it is a scandal that those whose chief professional
task is to interpret the biblical ground of the church's faith are,
in effect, illiterate. Again, there is little seriousness in many
pulpits in proclaiming the biblical form of the church's message.
The choosing of a text is a mere formality, a tradition without
direct relationship to the sermon. Presumably the function of
the text is to lend the nimbus of Divine authority to the clergyman's reflections of the past week. At all events, the alleged ex-
positor of the Word of God is rarely serious enough to pursue his
text into its original context.

Yet within the contemporary practice of the American pulpit there is an implicit, inchoate system of exegesis or interpretation — a system which contradicts the Protestant insistence on the literal or historical meaning of scripture as the basis of the church's theology and preaching. The harlot allegory and her exegetical handmaidens have returned in subtle disguises, and their charms are as beguiling as ever. They enable the church to transform the biblical faith into foreign categories, more useful to the church in its apologetic task, more intelligible and acceptable to men distant from the biblical age. The ugly, apocalyptic Christ is packaged as an attractive, modern product, which sells better. They enable the church to impart its own meanings to ancient revelation, to expand its supposed knowledge of God into the proportions grasped at in Eden and claimed by the comforters of Job. They enable the church so to manipulate God that He speaks as a dummy on the knee of the church.

How can the church speak honestly, disinterestedly, about God in proclaiming its faith? Honesty is not, of course, a simple possibility for fallen and sinful men. There are disciplines, however, by which the church may criticize its own language in speaking of God, controls by which we can cut away in part the incrustation of lies which obscures the biblical faith. These disciplines compose the theological enterprise. We confess that the truth or falsehood of our language about God must ultimately be judged by the revelation of God which constituted the Christian church, and by the direction of the Holy Spirit who guides the church. Hence, the theological enterprise is undertaken within the framework of a Christian theological school. At the same time, Christianity understands its revelation as indirect, a word mediated through historical event, to which ancient and modern men bear witness.

Thus the Christian doctrine of revelation is inevitably dialectical. The Bible, which the church confesses to be the Word of God, is at the same time the words of men, full of factual error, primitive ethics and bad theology. The Christ, which the church claims to be the Word of God incarnate, is at the same time a man, the creature of his times — mortal, finite, fallible. It is thus fitting that the theological enterprise be undertaken in the context of the secular university. For the language of the church about God must also fall under the judgment of nontheological disciplines — history, philosophy and science.

Let us take one example of a discipline born in the interaction between church and university, a discipline by which the language of the church about its God is challenged, cleansed, stripped of lies and dishonesty. Let us consider application of historical disciplines in the study of biblical religion.

Thanks to historical criticism, we can now trace the ironical fate of Job's dialogues, the process by which the book was twisted and tamed into a book more or less conformed to the interests of Jewish and Christian doctrine. And we can, by retracing the path, recover in part the freshness, vigor and offense of the original.

In the earliest stages of its transmission, Job's text fell into disarray; even with the full resources of modern historical scholarship, we still can read only about fifty per cent of its text with assurance. One reason for this textual corruption was simple ignorance on the part of early wisemen and scribes of the author's elevated literary language and erudite mythological allusions. Another reason, however, was the inability of these scribes to understand or even to read the text because of its unexpected unorthodoxy. Job has also been heavily interpolated; its dialogues were so much an offense that they could not be left unrevised. The defenders of the faith came off too badly. At some ancient time, therefore, a fourth friend (young Elihu) entered the picture and presented an alternate ending to the book. Fortunately, the same conservatism which introduced Elihu's speeches also preserved the original ending of the dialogues: the speeches of the Lord.

The guilt for the final perversion of the book lies on the heads of the later interpreters, translators and homilists. No corrupt text was left unturned in the search for Messianic allusions and references to resurrection. And the very point of the book was invented by students who located the "solution" of Job's problem in the folk tale which the author of the dialogue had chosen for his background.

As with Job, so with other books of the Old and New Testament: the tools and methods of modern historical research have removed the accretions formed by misunderstanding, reckless modernizing and false interpretation. The biblical writer is freed to speak his ancient words once again. Slowly we are learning to read the history of Israel and the primitive church as they actually developed. We are learning techniques and facts which will better enable us to place the religion of Israel in its pagan religious context, to detect its continuities with its environment and to define the traits which give it its own individuality, integrity and force.

As historical biblical study emerges within the theological enterprise, the task of the historian of biblical religion is being distinguished ever more carefully from that of the theologian. The distance between the religion of the Bible and the theology of the church becomes ever more apparent. A recognition of the distance between the biblical expression of the faith and the church's current language about God can be most beneficial. It can, for example, strip away the church's pretensions that its theology is simply biblical, or that it *can* be simply biblical. At the same time, it offers the theologian a new understanding of biblical materials by which the theological language of the church can be judged, purified and revised.

Ignoring these disciplines of historical research is a new form of dishonesty which we encounter in the modern church. Little teaching and less preaching give a hint that something has happened in biblical studies in the last two centuries. The deceit and futility of such "protectionist" procedures have been increasingly evident in recent years. The astonishing affair of the Qumrân scrolls is a dramatic illustration. Perhaps it is worth examining in some detail.

From the Qumrân scrolls have come a number of intimate parallels to early Christianity: its theology, its teachings, its understanding of history, its Messianism, its institutions, its language. The general reaction one would expect in the church is one of rejoicing. With such historical light, we can learn more of the primitive meaning of Christian institutions, improve New Testament interpretation and become more nearly contemporaries of Christ in our historical understanding. Yet the general reaction, as a matter of fact, is dismay. If there are parallels to Jesus' teachings and ministry, it is said, he is obviously not unique — and, therefore, not divine. The scrolls apparently prove that Christianity is simply another historical movement, growing organically out of its past, not revealed by God through His divine Son. If Christian institutions are not unique but existed in similar form in Judaism, people consider them somehow invalid.

Where do these notions come from? Is it possible that we have given the impression that Christianity was manufactured as a unit in heaven, a supernatural set of teachings and institutions unrelated to Israel's past or, for that matter, to the pagan world? Have we suggested, in our anxiety to promote the faith, that Christianity is not the continuation of the Old Testament faith and the fulfillment of the Judaism which that faith produced? No one should be surprised to learn from the Qumrân scrolls that Christianity is a Jewish sect. Our surprise is not that Christianity is Jewish, but that its relationships with a Jewish sectarian movement are, in many ways, more striking and even more illuminating than those with later Rabbinic Judaism.

What bearing do the Essene and other parallels to Jesus' ministry and teaching have on the Christian faith in Jesus as Messiah? Do they challenge the uniqueness of Jesus, or prove that he was not Messiah? This is not a new problem in Christian thought: In the nineteenth century, biblical criticism raised it in its most radical form — and theologians survive. For "uniqueness" is not an historical category. Every person or event is in one sense particular and unique. Yet no historical event can be disentangled from its historical causes; each emerges out of its past, continuous with it and dependent on it, and in this sense is not unique.

The "uniqueness" of Jesus is a dogmatic assertion, not an historical claim. When we attribute an event to Divine action, we properly do not call into question its normal continuity with other historical events nor its sources in human action. Few Christian theologies would deny that Jesus was determined by his historical environment and free within it, in the same sense that every man properly is. Jesus, in his own claims, insisted on the unity of his teaching with that of his past. His work was fulfillment, not innovation; he was obsessed, not with the enunciation of universal truths of religion, new or old, but with his role in the history of redemption. The Christian understands all this when he recites the orthodox formula that Jesus was true man.

If all this is true, why are church people troubled and restless over the Qumrân scrolls? Is it possible that we have protected our people from the truth, from the meaning of the humanity of Jesus? Have we made Jesus a remote God, mouthing teachings unknown before him, breaking into history and then escaping from it, untouched by its law and limitations? Have we so separated the Jesus of history from the Christ of faith that history is made meaningless, the eternal irrelevant?

Through our anxiety to magnify Jesus, to promote his teaching, to exalt the church at the expense of old Israel and to protect the brittle faith of comfortable congregations, we not infrequently become special pleaders for God. And in our dishonesty we deceive the people, pervert the faith, leave our sheep prey to the wolves of unbelief.

"Will you speak falsely for God?" Let me, for a moment, reverse the question: is it possible for men of our age to speak of the biblical God *without* lying?

I am not interested here in the problem of theological language. We have become very much aware of the precarious nature of our statements about God in the modern philosophic atmosphere. In one sense, it is true that all words spoken literally about God are false. We must use a language which points beyond itself, a symbolic language (or, I should prefer to say, the language of poetry) in describing the biblical God. We speak of the word of God and the act of God, but this word and this act are unlike any other word or act we hear or perceive. There is thus an element of deception in our language. One man drinks Christ's blood, and another is washed in it; one can scarcely choose between them. One claims that the Bible is the word of God and hence not the word of man; another that it is the word of man and hence not the word of God. Both lie in God's behalf. Much of the Bible is written in poetry, and much use is made of poetic saga, legend, myth. This is not by chance: the form is appropriate to the content. It would not have occurred to the prophet of Israel to preach except in poetry. It may be that our prosaic sermons which wither the altar flowers each Sunday morning are inevitably dishonest. In any case, the literalist who confuses saga with history, myth with science, poetry with prose, symbol with the symbolized, speaks falsely.

Nor am I interested, at least at the moment, in the problem of demythologizing our language about God. We seek to cleanse our language about God by discarding the ancient world view naïvely assumed by the biblical writer and replacing it with the modern world view which we naïvely assume. We swap a three-story universe for an expanding one, and Semitic psychology for Jung. Very good! But the problem is not a serious one.

I am concerned here, rather with the historical character of the biblical faith, especially its eschatological framework. Can the theologian or preacher retain the historical formulations of the biblical faith without lying for God? Can he still take seriously the biblical history of redemption?

Is it credible that God chose the people of Israel, that He is revealed in the concrete events of the Exodus? Is the Divine demand for justice revealed definitively in the Lord's delivering a community of slaves in the thirteenth century B.C.? And is God's purpose and human destiny revealed to us first of all in the establishment of the covenanted community, appointed to live in love, freedom and peace under His rule? Can we believe that, at a designated time, God chose Jesus as His Messiah and appointed the cross the means to free His community from the powers of sin and death? Can we take seriously the biblical narrative of the resurrection, by which God reveals the New Age dawning? And can we believe that the new epoch ushered in by the Christ will be consummated in a transformed humanity, living in perfect community in a new heaven and new earth?

The historical pattern of biblical religion cannot be ignored. The fact that historical and eschatological categories constitute the faith of Israel is seen more vividly with each advance of biblical criticism; and historical study of the New Testament reveals ever more clearly that an eschatological and apocalyptic framework gave unity and coherence to the early church's faith. Biblical religion is a theology of history. The modern theologian, as never before, must come to terms with the Bible's historical language about God.

The church's theologian may choose from several courses as he attempts to reformulate the biblical faith in terms meaningful in our age. He may attempt a primitivistic restoration of the eschatological language of the Bible in a modern theology. In this case, he may suppress the excessively mythological elements of the apocalyptic, since he wishes to retain only the historical element which transformed pagan myth into historical myth. He may also feel no responsibility to retain the flatly historical hopes of old Israel, since these are already reformulated in the eschatological poetry of the late prophets. But such a theological method is insufficiently radical and will produce merely another set of lies in God's behalf. Or rather, I should say that I cannot believe such language about God any longer, and I am persuaded that the modern man, not merely because of his corrupt state, finds it meaningless.

The modern man, like Job, views the flux of history in despair. He detects no pattern of meaning in history; it is a riddle beyond man's fathoming. The modern man, as scientist and historian, knows that he lived in no primeval age of innocence in the distant past. He knows that the earth and man will never be transformed in an historical cataclysm, but that the race will die and the planet turn into a cinder. He cannot believe in the resurrection of Jesus as a simple historical event; it offends him both as historian and as theologian. As the book of Job declares, God cannot be captured in history.

An alternative procedure for the theologian is to repudiate

the eschatological language of biblical religion. He then attempts to preserve biblical insights by transmuting them into categories drawn from modern mythologies or philosophical systems. These theological reformulations frankly dehistoricize biblical language. The term "historical" may be preserved, but its objective and subjective elements are carefully distinguished. The procedure is reminiscent of Solomon's proposal to cut in half a baby disputed by two mothers. If "historical" is analyzed into two parts, neither part remains "historical" in a biblical sense. The "historical" is murdered.

Perhaps dehistoricizing the faith is the only procedure left to the Protestant theologian who wishes to face honestly the distance between the biblical and the modern worlds. It is a radical operation, however, which removes from biblical religion that which gives it unity and form. Indeed, I am persuaded that the biblical revelation is inextricably bound in the historical, and that theologies which fail to come to terms with the eschatological structures of the biblical faith must sooner or later be set aside by the church.

Are these the only alternatives — a biblical theology which has become incredible, or a theology which has discarded the biblical understanding of history in order to become credible? I hope not, for either theology appears to fall short of the requirements that the church's language be both biblical and honest. Is there a third choice — a theological language which at once takes seriously the biblical doctrine of history and yet is intelligible and meaningful in the modern world? I hope so. To formulate such a language has been the perennial endeavor of the Protestant theologian and preacher. But at no time in the past has the task appeared so difficult and the need so great. I bid you join in this great theological enterprise with boldness and honesty of mind, and with fear and trembling.

The Pessimism of Ecclesiastes

by *Charles Conrad Forman*

The pessimism of Ecclesiastes has been an enigma to students of the Bible from the Council of Jamnia in A.D. 90 (when, it is said, Ecclesiastes was admitted to the canon on the strength of its interpolations!) to the present time. Critical scholarship has been concerned to find the source of Koheleth's pessimism. The issue resolves itself into two questions: is the pessimism due to Greek influence sullying the clear waters of Jewish orthodoxy, or is the author of Ecclesiastes a true son of the oriental spirit and mentality?

By way of introduction to the subject of this article it may be stated that the conclusion arrived at after extensive research in the wisdom literature is that there is nothing in Ecclesiastes demanding a frame of reference beyond the bounds of Semitic thought.[1] Careful examination of the wisdom writings of both Egypt and Mesopotamia has revealed ample materials comparable to the pessimistic utterances of the Preacher. We have also found that the Preacher naturally assumes a place in the evolution of Hebrew wisdom and that his pessimism springs from Semitic soil. Koheleth, indeed, is a son of the Orient and, in a special way, a true son of the Hebrews.

I

The prevailing opinion among scholars of the Old Testament has been that the pessimism of the book of Ecclesiastes must

---

(1) This paper was originally read before the Old Testament section of the Society of Biblical Literature and Exegesis in December 1956. It embodies some of the conclusions of a doctoral dissertation written under the direction of the late R. H. Pfeiffer, Hancock Professor of Hebrew and other Semitic Languages, which is now on deposit in the archives of Harvard University. The dissertation was entitled *Echoes of Ancient Pessimistic Thought in Ecclesiastes*.

Reprinted by permission of the author from Journal of Semitic Studies, *Vol. 3, No. 4, October 1958.*

be attributed to Greek influence, a point of view first advanced by Zirkel in 1792.[2] Zirkel based his conclusion on the discovery of alleged Grecisms in the *language* of Ecclesiastes, a view embraced by several critics in the nineteenth century.[3] The other line of influence defended by many critics is that the *thought* of our book shows traces of Greek contact.

The argument for Greek linguistic influence has, for the most part, been abandoned as an increased knowledge of the character of late Hebrew is gained. One of the strongest cases for Greek influence was the expression תחת השמש, which is said to occur twenty-eight times in Ecclesiastes. The phrase was paralleled with the Greek expression ὑφ' ἡλίῳ and appeared to be a legitimate identification until the same phrase was discovered in two Phoenician inscriptions of the third century B.C., thus providing the missing Semitic parallel to the Hebrew phrase. To be sure, it was occasionally still argued that the Phoenician evidence was, in effect, only further argument for the Greek, since Phoenician could have been indebted to the Greek at this point as at many others. More recently, however, the phrase "under the sun" has been found in Elamite inscriptions, giving conclusive evidence that the expression need not have been derived from Greek and, indeed, quite likely it was not.[4] Already in 1894 Paul Haupt observed that "the alleged Grecisms . . . are imaginary."[5] Recent scholarship bears him out in this judgment.

(2) *Untersuchungen über dem Prediger*, 1792.

(3) Representative of this point of view are the commentaries of the following: F. Hitzig, *Der Prediger Salomos erklärt*, 1847; P. Kleinert, *Der Prediger Solomo*, 1864; H. Graetz, *Koheleth*, 1871; T. Tyler, *Ecclesiastes — A Contribution to its Interpretation*, 1874; E. H. Plumptre, *Ecclesiastes*, 1881; O. Pfleiderer, *Die Philosophie des Heraclit von Ephesus, nebst Koheleth und besonders im Buch der Weisheit*, 1886; P. Haupt, *Koheleth, oder Weltschmerz in der Bibel*, 1905; also his *Book of Ecclesiastes*, 1905; G. Wildeboer, *Origin of the Old Testament Canon*, 1898; L. Levy, *Das Buch Koheleth*, 1912.

(4) Cf. J. Friedrich, *Orientalia*, xviii (1949), 28. I am indebted to Professor Cyrus H. Gordon of Brandeis University for calling this point to my attention. Cf. also his article "North Israelitic Influence on Postexilic Hebrew," *Israel Exploration J.* v (1955), 85-8.

(5) Paul Haupt, "The Book of Ecclesiastes," *Oriental Stud.*, 1894, p. 251.

The claim that Koheleth was influenced by the Greek philosophical schools and the gnomists has been defended most extensively in the studies of H. Ranston,[6] with noticeable effect on subsequent investigations of Koheleth. Unfortunately he begins with an unwarranted premise: namely, that Koheleth knew Greek. Space does not permit an examination of Ranston's thesis, but serious charges must be brought against those parts of his work built upon this assumption. From the most tentative parallels — and these extremely few in number — and from similarities of the most general kind and dealing with universal themes, he has advanced conclusions that are, to say the least, untenable. This is evident from the following statement, which asserts Greek influence as a fact rather than a suggestion: "In truth, the only religion left to Koheleth was but a mere shadow of the ancestral faith of his childhood; in both heart and head he is less a Jew than a Greek of the early gnomic type."[7]

II

In considering the points of similarity between any two peoples, one must not overlook the essential differences which are sometimes overshadowed by superficial likenesses. This is brilliantly illustrated in a penetrating lecture by S. H. Butcher entitled "Greece and Israel," where differences of ideas and mentalities are clearly drawn.[8] Professor Butcher first indicates points of comparison. In both peoples we find a spirit of universalism, the Greeks achieving it in the field of civilization while the Hebrews attained it in religion. Similarly, the Delphic religion and the Hebrew prophetic movement asserted moral claims upon their adherents, and the Fall of Man occurred in Greek thought with Prometheus' theft of fire just as it did in Genesis with the eating of the fruit of the tree of Knowledge. For both peoples, the Fall marked the end of the Golden Age.

---

(6) Cf. H. Ranston, *Ecclesiastes and the Early Greek Wisdom Literature,* 1925; "Ecclesiastes and Theognis," *American J. Semitic Languages,* xxxiv (1918) , 99-122; *The Old Testament Wisdom Books,* 1930.

(7) Ranston, *Old Testament Wisdom Books,* p. 286.

(8) S. H. Butcher, *Harvard Lectures on the Originality of Greece,* 1911, pp. 1-43.

But in spite of these similarities of thought, there are profound differences between the Hebrew and the Greek. There is a basic difference in the concept of man which may be seen in the fact that, while Prometheus is assured of immortality, Job is not; nor does Koheleth accept that doctrine, which makes its appearance only in the latest pages of the Old Testament. Another important point is that while Prometheus struggles against God, Job makes of his divine adversary an arbiter. While the Greeks had a somewhat exalted notion of man, the common Old Testament view was that he was a creature helpless apart from God. Finally, the concept of God is completely at variance in the two nations. The Greek was, in attitude and deed, intimately associated with his God; the Hebrew God became more and more transcendent. The God of the Hebrews revealed himself in history, while for the Greeks, with the exception of Herodotus, history had no meaning at all. But lest we be tempted to see Koheleth more essentially Greek than Hebrew in his interpretation of history, we must remember that he never denies meaning to history, but only maintains that its meaning escaped human understanding.

III

The evidence confirms the growing view of the scholarship of the last fifty years that there existed a community of thought in the ancient Near East in which Israel, like her neighbors, shared. The details of the mode of dissemination of these ideas are known only in the most general way, but cultural isolation for any nation in the Near East was well nigh impossible; exclusiveness notwithstanding, this applied to the Hebrews as much as to any other people, as their entire religious and political history illustrates. Koheleth, like other Hebrew writers, drew upon this common stock of ideas.[9]

It is, then, not surprising to find upon examination that the pessimism of Ecclesiastes shows characteristics common to the pessimism of Egypt, Mesopotamia and the Ahikar collection.

---

(9) Cf. Hugo Gressmann, *Israels Spruchweisheit in Zusammenhang der Weltliteratur*, 1925.

How much, and specifically which sayings, of Koheleth can be attributed to actual borrowings from any one of the Oriental sapiential writings, it is extremely difficult to ascertain. Furthermore, there is certainly much truth in the panoriental theory, which presupposes the gradual accumulation of a considerable body of material circulated in large measure in an oral form, thus making the identification of a precise quotation next to impossible.

Nevertheless, parallel ideas and similarities of expression found in *related* cultures render wholly unnecessary the need to look to another, *antagonistic* culture for evidence of the same sort in an attempt to prove influence. That Greek literature or philosophy is the source of Koheleth's striking departures from traditional thought is an unwarranted argument. Koheleth is much more at home in Israelite thought than has been generally supposed. He is first of all a Hebrew — though not orthodox — and he shares the same frame of reference and point of departure as his compatriots and coreligionists. His unorthodox conclusions do not take him out of an essentially Hebrew context; they merely emphasize a less apparent aspect of the thought of the Old Testament.

In another place we have attempted to show close patterns of thought and expression between the pessimistic passages in Ecclesiastes and the wisdom literature of the Egyptians, Akkadians and Hebrews.[10] Some of these comparisons are more striking than others, but in every case they support the thesis that Koheleth was a true son of the Near East and, most particularly, of Israel. The larger number of parallel passages show only the similarity of ideas that exist between the Preacher and his predecessors in the sapiential tradition. But the occasional similarity of expression cannot but cause us to wonder what, if any, of the literature of his neighbors he had come to know at first hand. Baumgartner, Galling and Humbert agree in arguing for an Egyptian influence greater than any other in Ecclesiastes.[11]

---

(10) Cf. chs. iv, v, vi of dissertation mentioned above, n. i.
(11) Cf., Walter Baumgartner, *Israelitische und Altorientalische Weisheit,* 1933; Kurt Galling and Max Haller, *Die Fünf Megilloth,* 1940; Paul Humbert, *Recherches sur les Sources Egyptiennes de la Littérature Sapientiale d'Israël,* 1925.

While we cannot agree that there is any serious evidence for claiming Alexandria as the place of origin, as both Humbert and Galling suggest, we must agree that the evidence for Egyptian influence in Koheleth is incontrovertible.

While the materials are not as abundant for comparing Babylonian and Assyrian literature of the *hokmah* variety as they are for the Egyptian, there is, nevertheless, sufficient material to show that Koheleth had some acquaintance with it. In some form he must have known *Gilgamesh,* or at least been acquainted with some of the ideas that had their origin in the epic and became the common property of Near Eastern speculation. Likewise, the teachings regarding the nature of man and the relationship of men and the gods in the Akkadian proverbial literature show themselves to be in close harmony with Koheleth.

The speculative cuneiform writings (e.g. the *Babylonian Job,* the *Pessimistic Dialogue Between Master and Servant* and *A Dialogue about Human Misery,* often called the *Babylonian Koheleth*) deal with the same problem of human goals, the meaning of life and the fact of death. One cannot read far in this group of writings without being struck by the compatibility of mood and conclusion between them and the Hebrew Ecclesiastes. In one way or another, they are all of a kind, possessing a profound unity of thought. While the evidence of the relationship between Koheleth and the Akkadian sages is wanting as regards the details of the acquaintance of the former with the latter, it is nevertheless obvious that some degree of familiarity is certain.

IV

But the great single source of Koheleth's pessimism is to be found in the Hebraic tradition of thought and speculation. It is within this Israelitic framework that Koheleth thought and re-thought the assertions of religion, and from that tradition he accepted or rejected given propositions as the evidence he gathered confirmed or denied those claims. To the *S document* of Genesis Koheleth was attracted and heavily indebted. This is especially true in the Preacher's concept of God, where, as in Genesis, God is both omnipotent and hostile. In both books

God creates man of dust; and to limit the power of man he imposes upon him toil (only in Genesis it is physical while in Ecclesiastes it is intellectual toil!); and finally, death is the sentence decreed for all creatures. Man is overpowered by the hunger for knowledge in Genesis; in Ecclesiastes the same restless, searching spirit is manifest. But in the latter there is no comfort derived from the fruits of knowledge, for what knowledge does come to man only further reveals his creaturely limitations and the insignificance of his place in the universe. Pedersen has aptly observed that "the misfortune of Ecclesiastes is that the horizons under which he lived as an Israelite were shattered. He discovered that nature does not exist in a special way for man."[12]

The influence of the book of Proverbs on Koheleth is not great except in a negative manner. Proverbs is permeated with a scheme of life that oversimplifies the issues at stake. Koheleth seized upon one or another of the assertions of Proverbs to disclaim it, merely by putting over against it the evidence of life as the latter is seen and experienced.[13]

The book of Job represents another significant influence on Ecclesiastes, for Job raised the questions that were to expose the implications of Hebrew transcendence. Did God really care for righteousness? If he did, then was he helpless to reward it? Job concluded that God was indeed omnipotent — but was he good as men understand goodness? In a sense Koheleth begins where Job leaves off, for he accepts the omnipotence of God and discards any claim of divine goodness. God is unfriendly and withdrawn. As Pfeiffer has said: "God's hostility to men is even more pronounced [in Ecc.] than in the myths of Genesis 2-3 and 11,

---

(12) Johannes Pedersen, *Scepticisme Israélite*, 1931, p. 29.

(13) The same negative evidence was the result in examining the Wisdom Psalms and even more so in Ben Sira. In the case of the latter, I am aware that the majority of students would place Ben Sira after Koheleth. I do not, however, believe that the question is finally settled, nor can it be until more evidence is available. In any case, Ecc. and Ecclus. are very close and Ecclus. was studied merely as a possible source of Ecc.

and in the Book of Job. . . ."[14] In both Job and Koheleth (as indeed in *S*, although it is not stressed there except in the story of creation), God is the first cause, and the doctrine of causality must inevitably lead to determinism and thus to pessimism. Ecclesiastes provides all the illustration we need of the implications of the Hebrew conception of omnipotence when restraints of morality or justice or mercy are removed. Again, both Job and Koheleth deal with the quest for wisdom, and both conclude that wisdom is inaccessible to human minds.

In addition to the influence on Ecclesiastes of the specific books we have mentioned, a further word must be said on the effect of the doctrine of retribution. Koheleth rejected this teaching, deep-seated as it was in the religious thinking of Israel, because it was contradicted in human experience; he thus denied divine justice, which was inevitably a corollary to the theory of reward and punishment. But Koheleth rejected this doctrine on other grounds too. The promises of orthodoxy, even if they should prove to be true, as in individual instances they did, were not satisfactory. Wealth was vanity; and ultimately life — even long life — was vanity, for there was no alternative to the inevitability of death. Thus the tenets of orthodoxy, even when taken at face value, were rendered meaningless by a careful evaluation of the rewards that were guaranteed the righteous, for they were empty rewards, of the substance of wind.

The only adequate explanation of the origin of the pessimism of Ecclesiastes must be found within the Hebraic tradition. Breasted's account of the cause of scepticism in Egyptian letters of the Feudal Age applies extremely well to the scepticism which grew up in Israel and came to full flower in the teaching of Koheleth. He wrote:

Scepticism means a long experience with inherited beliefs, much rumination on what has heretofore received unthinking acquiescence, a conscious recognition of personal power to believe or disbelieve, and thus a distinct step forward in the development of self-consciousness and personal initiative. It is only a people

(14) "The Peculiar Skepticism of Ecclesiastes," *J.B.L.* LIII (1934), 102f.

of ripe civilization who develop scepticism. It is never found under primitive conditions. It was a momentous thousand years of intellectual progress, therefore, of which these sceptics of the Feudal Age represented the culmination.[15]

Pedersen says the same thing when he observes that "pessimism" and scepticism belong to the advanced periods in the life of a people."[16] New influences do not produce pessimism, but the denial of old tenets of life and faith most assuredly do result in pessimism, unless with the denial there is a positive affirmation from which a reconstruction may be made. Suddenly there were for Koheleth no goals for life, no purposes that counted significantly. In this negation we have the starting point for understanding the thought of the Preacher. This is the source of the pessimism of Ecclesiastes.

---

(15) J. H. Breasted, *Development of Religion and Thought in Ancient Egypt,* 1912, p. 181.

(16) Pedersen, *op. cit.,* p. 15.

A Doctrine for Our Times

by Robert B. Tapp

We live in a world changing so fast that most of us were already out-of-date when we left school. We live in the midst of a liberal church changing faster than we can comprehend or guide it. It is a rare scanner of the signs of these times who can discern the difference between midnight and morning, or even assure us that day inevitably follows night.

Many among us have succumbed to that peculiar malady of our epoch — the anxiety over not being anxious. As Gilbert Murray said of the late Romans and as Sidney Hook said of the late New Dealers, we have experienced a failure of nerve. Few things will be more puzzling to our future historians than the eagerness with which many in our liberal camp have listened to what "they" (Tillich, the Niebuhrs, Barth, Brunner, *et al.*) have been saying about "us" — not only listened, as all of us should, but *agreed!* When did you last hear, or preach, a sermon about liberalism's "loss of a dimension of depth"? Or about "ontological shock"? Or about the recovery of a sense of "human sinfulness"? Or about "the existential" — that blessed barbarism which has replaced our former adjectives "real" and "true"?

Please don't misunderstand me. I *believe* in sin. And I think the closest example of it is the failure of our liberal officialdom and seminaries in recent decades to preserve a lively theological sophistication about our theological traditions and the history of liberalism. Only such a gross sin could have left so many of us so unprepared to distinguish between the winds of doctrine and the hot airs that buffet us. But a corporate confession of this sin does not require us to return to some neo-Protestant confessionalism.

In fact, I suspect that quite the reverse will be the case. The brief for modern man, which we helped to write, is a pretty good one. Our problems, on second look, seem more to stem from a lack of modernity than from a surfeit.

I, for one, am still something of an optimist about the human estate. I still find a basic goodness in the human animal — a goodness which is not meaningfully qualified or negated by references to a "fall," even a mythical one. I am also forced to trace a progress in human history which undergirds a realistic optimism. Nor do I find my adopted ancestors *really* talking about any automatic escalator to eternity.

Finally, and more central to the faith of our fathers, I still find it more useful to speak of human reason than of any other functioning of our being. How else shall we discuss our feelings of truth and beauty and goodness but by reason? These matters do not, as some would say, defy discussion. Our community, our church, is grounded in just such communication.

Even as a non-Freudian, I am jarred to hear Freud imprecated in defense of irrationalism. Of course there are irrational elements in our experience of ourselves and, seemingly, of our cosmos. But to comprehend them, to understand them, perhaps even to control them — how else but by reason?

And time, it would seem, is on our side. Never in history has a small movement, which ours surely is, had so many powerful allies. Every new breakthrough in the sciences underscores our faith in the reach of reason. Every new schoolchild is a harbinger of a larger harvest of the developed human mind. Every advance in welfare-stateism, even under tyrannical auspices, moves another group of our brothers closer to what Professor Karl Deutsch has called the "take-off point" — the point at which men are sufficiently freed from the pressures of their environment to impress their own wills upon it.

With such allies, how can we lose? Time and history are on our side. But Strontium-90, I must remind myself, is also in the race. My vision is not of what will be, but of what may be. Are there not, however, good evidences that ordinary people, given some information, are often wiser than their statesmen — or at least than their generals and admirals?

What is the vision? An exciting new world, even if not necessarily a brave one. Religious liberals are called, not to save it from itself, but to guide it into being fully itself. And their

allies will be many. Our danger is not that we will be too far in
the van, but that we will be passed by. Nothing is so irrelevant
as outmoded fact, warmed over and served up as today's faith.
A religious liberal who is still wedded to yesterday's truths has
become orthodox without knowing it. I recently listened in on a
conversation between a young psychiatrist, who was sympatheti-
cally exploring some aspects of extrasensory perception and faith
healing, and one of our theological professors, who was know-
ingly the scoffer in the name of "science."

We can lose our relevance to these times, not by being
wrong, but by being insufficiently and inadequately right. Our
times are moving, and they are moving in general directions that
historic liberalism has pointed. To stay on the crest of a wave,
one must paddle — with wisdom and with skill.

The price of relevance is neither more members nor more
friends. Our major needs can be discussed under three headings:

1 —— We need an *adequate theological sensitivity.* Contrary to much of what may be heard about us, even within our
own circles, liberalism is not the obverse of orthodoxy. Rather,
we differ in our starting points. We begin with an assessment
of man and his potential. While this is not necessarily the opposite of "God's mighty acts," we have found it a more fruitful
approach.

If we have been correct in this approach, then supernaturalism is ruled out. However, liberal theologizing has been grounded
in both naturalistic and idealistic philosophies, and these remain
as present options. Regardless of the approach, the liberal concern from Socrates to our times has ultimately been with excellence (*arete*) in the whole human animal. Perhaps theology
might even be called a science, from this point of view, in its
attempt to conceptualize *both* what has been and what is coming
to be. We might even call the interplay of these two approaches
— that based on the recognized characteristics of man, and that
based on his emergent tendencies — *agapics,* using a Greek root
for "love" that was prominent in early Christian times. The
hypothesis of agapics is that altruistic love is a *fact,* that it func-

tions creatively in human development, and even in evolution. Agapics can thus describe the whole man, functioning fully, much as the physician's concept "health" describes both the present state of the body and its general tendency of development.

If we come at the matter this way, we shall avoid two pitfalls. We shall not be denying that empirical, rational inquiry can deal with human goods and values. In today's scene, this is no small accomplishment. On the other hand, and equally important, we shall avoid expecting our scientists and technicians to *produce* values through research. Values are made by men, are relevant as they reshape life and inquiry, and are open to useful study only when they do just that.

2 —— Our second need is now apparent. If the shaping and achieving of those values that fulfill human potentialities is at the center of liberal theology, then the church has a clear function quite apart from purely intellectual pursuits. It is the laboratory in which these values are sought, tested and nourished. Thus a prime need is a more profound worship — that is, *a deepening of the relationship between belief and practice.*

Worship, as most of us understand it, is that mode of experience in which the whole of our being responds to the claims of reality upon us. This can happen both in our solitude and in our group life. Yet our actual behavior on this level is embarrassingly haphazard and shallow. Whether we proclaim brotherhood or integrity or dignity or democracy, the gap between theory and behavior is glaring.

Most of us would agree that the process of being intrigued and jolted and remade by these values involves a form of worship. But how many of us are genuinely intrigued, or jolted or remade? If the worship is to be valid, all the richness of mind and emotion must be stirred. To this end, we must utilize all the arts (including the ultimate art of sensing what is central.)

The fact that the psychology of religion has uncovered so much that is unhealthy or undesirable among church members further underscores this crucial relationship between belief and practice. Can a liberal church, which rejects trivial and pathological beliefs and holds to the profoundly simple belief in creative love, prove that such love can be developed by education? And, of supreme importance, can it prove that the liberal church is the best vehicle for such education?

To do so, we must heed more carefully all that the psycho-therapists have discovered in their attempts to bring alienated persons back into contact. We must study most closely the phe-nomenon of resistance, which plays such a central part in so much of genuinely religious experience. It may be that the most de-sirable values are also the hardest to obtain and that this very fact makes their claims upon us so threatening. Peter was neither the first nor the last to say, "Depart from me, for I am a sinful man." The line between humility and timidity is a fine one.

Most of us, most of the time, are exceedingly ambivalent about our central values. Let us accept this, as a start. Then let us go on to create and inhabit those structures which can move us beyond vacillation and rationalization into more integral living. The church can be such a structure when it lives under constant criticism, from without and within. The problem is to know what we really want to achieve in terms of human poten-tialities. The answers will never be fixed, nor will the goals; but we can gain the vision to see directions and next steps.

3 —— This leads to the final need — the need for an *adequate social ethic.* There are still disadvantaged persons and groups in our society, and any sensitive religious group must be responsive to the demands of justice. But we must distinguish carefully between the work done and the work to be done. Our support of racial integration, for instance, is for all practical purposes unanimous. No new theories seem necessary, simply the persistent and persuasive application of what we already know. One might almost say that brotherhood is in America today a legal, economic and educational problem: ethical pioneering is no longer called for.

This is true of many of the old "causes." There is no sadder sight than alleged liberals trying in our day to assume the radical postures of the 1930s. Nor must we neglect the lessons of the last two decades and succumb to the easy tendency to focus on the environment, while ignoring the individuals who make up such a large part of it. The tired and bitter reformer, whose being betrays his program, needs a psychiatrist more than he needs a pulpit.

An adequate social ethic in our day will address itself to the *advantaged* groups. It will jar their complacency and confusion about themselves. What *are* the effects of an economy of consumption? What are the moral privileges (and pitfalls) of the age of affluence? For what does less — and less tedious — work free us? How does one find meaning in a lengthened life span, if a short life has already been boring and uncreative? In a large society, where power is depersonalized and organizations proliferate, how can the individual hope to see some of his values incorporated into the massive realities? Most puzzling of all, how can reason operate to check the drift into a war that no one wants and whose outcome will be genetically disastrous, quite apart from any short-term political results?

None of these questions is wholly new. Certainly none has received serious consideration, or achieved even minimal clarification, in our liberal community. Yet these are some of today's issues; and we must face these issues and weave them into our interpretation of the potentialities of human society. For such a venture, no lines can be drawn between our religious and our secular neighbors. These are questions where fact and value merge and, therefore, where all dogmatism is predoomed to fail.

In outlining our needs in the areas of theological thinking, practical implementation and ethical sensitivity, I have actually been calling for a new doctrine of the liberal church. That we now lack such a doctrine should be apparent to all. That no one can authoritatively hand us such a doctrine should be equally clear. That cooperative inquiry might lead us into a greater consensus and therefore a greater effectiveness is but a hope. It seems, however, to be a hope that reasonable men may and must reasonably entertain.

Falling Away from Greatness

by Norman Livergood

The perspective from which I write is that of one outside the fold of Unitarianism looking appreciatively within. My thinking in this area derives not only from a study of theology, but also from personal experience as a minister of Protestant churches for some years.

My study of Unitarian tradition and history has impressed me with the strength and truth of the movement. Its great figures from the time of Servetus stir me to similar zeal and like understanding. But a study of contemporary Unitarianism leaves a disappointing impression: there appears a glaring inconsistency between its liberal profession and its most conservative practice. One expects to find evidence of the progressive, forthright beliefs of Unitarianism manifesting themselves in bold, creative activities and programs. One finds, instead, relatively orthodox methods of organization, practice and worship.

Had Unitarianism fulfilled its earlier promise it would today stand in sharper contrast to Protestant orthodoxy and offer a more worthy alternative to the religious world. On the basis of Unitarian *history,* a religious liberal could well take his place within the movement. But present Unitarian *practice* seems scarcely more progressive or challenging than does orthodoxy.

Let us consider three areas in which change might strengthen Unitarianism and bring it into closer reach of its great potentialities.

A local church letter (which had best remain anonymous) illustrates the contemporary opinion of some Unitarian churches concerning evangelism or proclamation:

It is our aim to keep membership on the same level as the ideals of the Church itself. That is, we want it to be a free choice of the individual. Thus we do not urge people to join. We do, however, most cordially invite those who feel their kinship with

121

us to enter into the relation of formal membership that together we may meet the obligations which our freedom imposes on us.

I believe this statement arises from a misunderstanding of evangelism. Confronting another person with one's position is not necessarily coercion, and urging involves no abridgment of freedom. The church's modest attitude naïvely assumes that there are no urges already present, when life is, in fact, full of persuasions, subtle and direct. Unitarianism has rightly revolted against the older type of evangelism, in which one sect sought to convert the world to its own peculiar dogma or ecclesiastical form, or sought to "Christianize" the world. But in reacting against this, it has gone to the opposite extreme and excluded almost all evangelism.

Promulgation of one's convictions is a vital part of faith. The sanctity of another's freedom is not thereby destroyed. Intellectual and academic circles are famous for free exchange of opinion. To stay outside the arena of personal opinion, making no appeal to others, is to misread human nature. People make decisions only after the issues and choices are clearly presented. To wait until people come asking about Unitarianism suggests not so much liberalism as misunderstanding and lack of adequate fervor.

Perhaps the greatest sermon preached from an evangelistic yet liberal point of view is William Ellery Channing's famous discourse, "Unitarian Christianity Most Favorable to Piety." Preached in 1826, this sermon was an effort to *proclaim* Unitarianism and the value of a liberal faith.

Boston was at that time the location of an active revival of orthodoxy. Many orthodox ministers were saying that Unitarianism was too cold and intellectual to be effective as a religious faith (a charge still often heard). Channing's reply was a vigorous presentation of the reasons for choosing Unitarianism above all other traditions. Speaking from absolute conviction, Channing was truly and nobly evangelistic. He believed Unitarianism was the finest expression of religious devotion, and felt compelled to promulgate his belief. This same impulse could and should impel modern Unitarians to give expression and voice to their faith.

Perhaps the most outstanding contribution of contemporary Unitarianism, and that most deserving publicity and appreciation, is its work in religious education. The activity in this field is a truly creative accomplishment. If each point of its faith were so reflected in appropriate structures and activities, Unitarianism would more nearly fulfill its potentiality. The achievements in this field by Unitarians deserve and call for evangelism.

A projection made by the Unitarian Commission of Appraisal in 1936 expresses the second major challenge:

Avoiding with the utmost care any suggestion of any official creed, and insisting at every point upon the right of minorities, majorities, and the total group, to change their minds as knowledge advances, they will nevertheless be unafraid to say with some real degree of definiteness, "These are things which today we believe to be true." They will realize that they may believe differently tomorrow, and therefore will not set up any credal test for membership in their church; but they will affirm, with conviction, that they hold this body of doctrine at the present moment; and they will regard it as of great importance to formulate thus from time to time the varying stages of their growing belief so that it may serve as the basis for worship, ethics, and program.[1]

A clear theology should be outlined by every new generation of Unitarians. In the attempt to avoid creeds, the denomination has — as with evangelism — moved to an extreme position. An outline of beliefs does not necessarily function as a creedal requirement for membership; it can stand as a tentative statement which gives clarity and definitude. There is much benefit to be derived from such a statement: it moves people away from uncertainty, which breeds indifference; it meets the spiritual needs of those who want to belong to a group that stands for something openly; it makes for a church not a discussion group; it inspires

(1) *Unitarians Face a New Age,* Commission of Appraisal, American Unitarian Assoc., Boston, Beacon Press, 1936, p. 7.

to further study by giving a solid basis upon which to build; and it acts as a unifying force drawing all of like mind together.

Membership in a Unitarian church should mean something definite. As the Commission declared:

> To be sure, there may be a few persons on the outer edge of the fellowship who will regard such an attempt to formulate doctrinal agreements and disagreements as a valid reason for withdrawing. . . . If the only condition on which such persons will remain in the fellowship is that Unitarianism should stand for nothing — or at any rate nothing definite — in the realm of religious thought and belief, then it might be gain rather than loss to violate that condition.[2]

Unitarianism has historically been a movement of thinking people — people who came to this faith by virtue of definite conviction. Modern Unitarianism, however, has become a congeries of confused opinions and vague beliefs.

In trying to be inclusive, Unitarianism has fallen into the error of vacuity; its attempt to encompass all types of faith has been at the cost of precision. It is amazing how many people unknowingly believe indefiniteness to be a virtue in religion.

Perhaps the epitome of clarity and explicitness is Dr. Channing's famous sermon on "Unitarian Christianity":

> We regard the Scriptures as the records of God's successive revelations to mankind, and particularly of the last, and most perfect revelation of his will by Jesus Christ. . . .
> . . . we believe in the doctrine of God's UNITY, or that there is one God, and one only. . . .
> We believe that Jesus is one mind, one soul, one being, as truly one as we are, and equally distinct from the one God. . . .
> We believe in the *moral perfection of God*. We consider no part of theology so important as that which treats of God's moral character. . . .
> We earnestly maintain that Jesus, instead of calling forth, in any way or degree, the mercy of the Father, was sent by that mercy to be our Saviour; that he is nothing to the human race but what he is by God's appointment; that he communicates nothing but what God empowers him to bestow; that our Father in heaven is

(2) *Ibid.*, p. 34.

originally, essentially, and eternally placable, and disposed to forgive; and that his unborrowed, underived, and unchangeable love is the only fountain of what flows to us through his Son. . . .

We believe that all virtue has its foundation in the moral nature of man, that is, in conscience, or his sense of duty, and in the power of forming his temper and life according to conscience.[3]

The same major challenge — the challenge to a decisive theological position — has been acutely expressed by James Luther Adams:

The expansive, assimilative tendency in liberalism which has enriched it has also flattened it out into a vague, indefinite *omnium gatherum* of watered-down truths selected at random from the various religious traditions and secular movements which have happened to elicit attention. The belief in the so-called "wider view" which transcends all particular traditions has in many cases resulted only in an amorphous, mystical secularism and has produced a liberalism which possesses no indigenous tradition, literature or language. It has even detached many people from Christianity, the one tradition which they have some capacity for knowing from the inside. Consequently, though much of contemporary liberalism is cosmopolitan and comprehensive (and we should hope it will continue to be so), it is at the same time rootless and lacking in that concentration which alone can give it distinction and character. For this reason, it is difficult for many people to see what difference it makes to be a liberal. No particular body of religious literature, no religious language is recognized as characteristic of religious liberalism; and no set of disciplines is generally considered to be incumbent upon the adherent of our faith.[4]

One of the most important areas of contemporary theological discussion is the doctrine of man. This is the chief area of attack upon liberalism by orthodoxy and neo-orthodoxy. Orthodox criticism, however, is unjustified and misdirected: it opposes a "liberal" concept of man which never existed in any scheme of

---

(3) *The Works of William E. Channing*, Boston, American Unitarian Assoc., 1875, pp. 367-80.

(4) J. L. Adams, "The Liberalism that is Dead," *Journal of Liberal Religion*, Winter 1940, pp. 1-2.

thought. Philosopher Brand Blanshard has approached a clear definition of the liberal position on this doctrine:

> If "perfectibility" means the capacity to be perfect, and "progress" means the inevitability of progress, no instructed liberal ever believed in either. If they mean that by devoted effort we can make ourselves and our world enormously better, which is all that liberals claim, . . . [the neo-orthodox] is doing no service in denying such convictions.[5]

Another pressing issue which faces contemporary Unitarians is the decision whether to remain exclusively Christian or to adopt a different position somewhere nearer to humanism. The lack of decision on this basic question has given indistinctness to Unitarianism for some decades. And this issue is just one of a myriad of similar questions still undecided and unanswered by modern Unitarianism. Until it has arrived at an explicit statement of opinion on these issues, it cannot hope for vital unity or clear understanding by others.

The third challenge was set forth succinctly in 1936 by the Commission of Appraisal:

> In the present conflict of social forces, [liberal churches] will take sides openly whenever the ideals of liberalism are in peril, and they will throw the weight of their influence on the side of every agency which seeks to promote human welfare by methods consistent with their religion.[6]

The genius of Unitarianism has always been its candid expression of a liberal faith. This element seems largely to have been lost by the contemporary movement. There is little ferment of ideas entering the public stream of discourse from Unitarianism. Its people seem to have given up the dynamic of debate and, like other religious groups, have drawn back into themselves, content with shallow discussion and easy criticism. This is a great

---

(5) Brand Blanshard, "The Theology of Power," *The Nation,* March 22, 1958, p. 254.
(6) *Op. cit.,* p. 8.

loss; free debate is an integral part of liberal faith, and the loss of
it leads to weakness.

The history of Unitarianism rings with debate. Since Servetus, as a youth, took up its torch against the leaders of the
Reformation, debate has served a most useful purpose. In 1569
a king was won to Unitarianism by the force of persuasive argument. The Trinitarian Controversy in England saw Unitarians
challenging the orthodox to public discourse. If the Unitarianism
of the twentieth century is to live up to its past, it must enter
again the arena of truth and speak for its liberal faith.

Much in Unitarianism today gives great promise for the
growth and development of its potential. Its liberal ideal can
be developed, reorganized and revitalized so as to come well within striking distance of its potentialities. This will, however,
involve changes that are deep-cutting. It will require a large
measure of courage and determination to carry such a program
through to success.

But until Unitarianism can more nearly realize its great
possibilities, it will offer little advance to those who search for a
liberal religious faith. By refusing to evolve beyond the binding
limits of its orthodox structures, it is failing its own ideal. By
again looking to its great past, by drawing strength from its
figures of genius in this and previous ages, it can become a movement to challenge the spirit and mind of men.

Man, God and Space

by Arthur Foote

Go not, my soul, in search of him; thou wilt not find him there —
Or in the depths of shadow dim, or heights of upper air.
For not in far-off realms of space the Spirit hath its throne;
In ev'ry heart it findeth place and waiteth to be known.
— Frederick Lucian Hosmer

Whatever the Russians, Americans or anybody else may find "in far-off realms of space" with their moon-girdling, sun-orbiting manmade satellites, no one, I suspect, will quarrel with Hosmer: man will not find God out there. Our spaceships may report fabulous new discoveries concerning the chemical constitution of the cosmos. They may force abandonment of scientific hypotheses long considered axiomatic. But does anyone seriously expect these manmade invaders into outer space to stumble upon the location of heaven or the throne of God?

We humans find ourselves plummeting into the Atomic Age — an age in which the frontiers of human knowledge are expanding at a bewildering tempo. We are in the midst of an industrial revolution which quite dwarfs that of the eighteenth and nineteenth centuries. A few years ago, the Second International Conference on Atomic Energy was held at Geneva, attended by five thousand leading scientists — certainly the largest group of top world scientists ever brought under one roof. Seventy-three countries were represented, and more than two thousand technical papers were presented.

If dramatic evidence of the speed with which humanity is plunging into this new epoch were needed, this great conference would amply provide it. Man is rapidly learning "to harness and utilize directly the cosmic energy which surrounds him in profuse abundance."

Where all this is taking us, only a Jules Verne would venture to predict. But a few things do seem clearly predictable. One is that we must choose between war and survival. Unless mankind can achieve peace, securely founded on world law, and turn its full and undivided attention toward solving the problems of survival, the chances seem to be ninety-nine to one that earth will shortly end a burned-up cinder, devoid of sentient life.

Another relatively safe prediction is that, barring a world-wide catastrophe, the human population will continue to mushroom at an alarming rate. Within a century there will be four or five billion of us. Next to the abolition of war, mankind has perhaps no greater problem than achieving, through effective international machinery, a stabilization of the world's population.

Another fact of great importance is that modern man is living far beyond his global means, far beyond earth's ability to support him. In their selfish greed and shortsighted wastefulness, men have pillaged the earth's resources butchering her forests and allowing her fertile topsoil to wash and blow away. It is common knowledge that, with a doubling of the world's population, the known resources of fossil fuels will be exhausted within the next century.

Scientists measure the total consumption of energy in immense units called "Q"s. A Q is equal to a million million million British thermal units — or the amount of energy produced by the consumption of thirty-three thousand million tons of coal. Until the year 1800, mankind consumed the earth's stored-up energy of coal, oil and waterpower at the rate of about one-half Q per century. By the beginning of the atomic era, the rate of consumption had become twenty times as great — one Q every decade — so effectively have we learned to use the stored-up energy of the sun, poured onto the earth during many millions of years, to increase our comfort and enrich our leisure.

But mankind, like an individual, can live beyond its means only until its capital is gone. However unready in other ways — such as social and moral development — man may have been coping with atomic energy, in one sense at least the discovery may have come just in time to save the race from planetary bankruptcy. Only by learning how to utilize directly cosmic energy can the race continue its global industrialization and fulfill its fabulous dreams of universal economic abundance.

The Atomic Age, the Space Age, seems destined to see the transformation of the outward, physical, material life of man. It also presents him with the very stern challenge to grow up, to transform himself, to achieve a far greater ethical maturity than he has yet known. Indeed, it was never truer that "wisdom is the principal thing . . . and with all thy getting get understanding."

The religious implications of the Space Age are many. One of them is that man needs to re-evaluate his place in the cosmos. The unknown poet of Genesis could write that God created the earth, then the sun and the moon, and finally add almost as an afterthought: "He made the stars also." But we know that the earth is not the focal point of creation. Copernicus forced abandonment of the geocentric theory, and our ancestors had painfully to recognize that earth was but one of a handful of planets circling the sun. But that was only the beginning of the cosmic readjustment, a readjustment we are yet far from having completely made. For, of course, the sun is no more the center of the universe than is the earth.

The author of Genesis thought there were but a few thousand stars, those visible to the naked eye. Galileo and Newton's telescopes multiplied the known number to a million or more. In our childhood, a generation ago, men thought there were several billion stars. Today's estimate is that there are more than one hundred thousand million billion flaming suns.

Our solar system is "one lost feather of light" in a faint spiral arm on the fringe of an ordinary galaxy, the Milky Way. As Harlow Shapley of Harvard observed in his recent book *Of Stars and Men:* "We must get used to the fact that we are peripheral, that we move along with our star, the sun, in the outer part of a galaxy that is one among billions of star-rich galaxies."[1] If man has any claim to cosmic significance, says this learned

(1)   Boston, Beacon Press, 1958, p. 9.

astronomer, it certainly isn't to be discovered in his location in space, or in time, or in his chemical composition. We, like all animals, are made of the same stuff as our earth and our sun — a handful of chemicals common throughout the cosmos.

It is not only the incredible immensity of the universe — in which our nearest stellar neighbor, Alpha Centauri, is some twenty-five trillion miles away — which should force us to re-evaluate man's place and cosmic significance. We also face the fact that the origin of life itself is no longer an insoluble mystery, something to be accounted for only by miraculous supernatural intervention. "We have bridged," says Shapley, "at least provisionally, the gap between life and the lifeless. The microbiologist probing down from cells toward the inanimate and the chemist moving up from atoms toward the animate are practically in contact."[2]

There simply is no need, any longer, for the hypothesis of a supernatural deity, a creative agent intervening from the outside. Entirely natural processes suffice.

There is an additional consideration, which can serve as a valuable corrective to our human egotism. This is the high probability that the earth is not the only location of life in the universe. True, man cannot yet demonstrate the existence of other planetary systems sustaining organic life. Perhaps he never will be able to, since even the nearest stars are so remote. But leading astronomers are coming to accept quite generally the thesis that, in all probability, there are many planets beyond our solar system where life can and presumably does exist.

Man, argues Professor Shapley, should accept as by far the most reasonable hypothesis the notion that there is an abundance of habitable planets. Remember, he says, that our sun is an entirely ordinary sort of star, very much the common garden variety. One hundred thousand of the million brightest stars are essentially identical to it — in size, in luminosity, in motion and in chemical composition.

Remember also that our universe is an expanding one. The

(2) *Ibid.*, p. 14.

evidence is well-established that the galaxies, like Caesar on his horse, are tearing away from each other in all directions; and the time must have been (a few billion years ago) when the galaxies were close together — intermingled, overlapping, colliding. It was then, astronomers think, that stellar accidents were frequent and innumerable planetary systems came violently into being.

Not all planets, of course, provide opportunity for life. To support life, a planet must orbit its sun stably at the right distance to maintain sufficiently moderate temperatures. It must collect to itself a nonpoisonous atmosphere, and so forth. But even when we have listed every conceivable restriction, and reduced to a minimum the number of planets we think might meet all the conditions for sentient life, we are left with a large figure.

We must also remember, says Shapley, that all the evidence points to the universality of the kind of chemistry and physics we know here; and, finally, that there are more than one hundred thousand million billion stars. Even if only one star in a billion has a planet so situated as to be hospitable to life — far too conservative a figure, says Shapley — we still are left with a hundred million earths scattered through space where the conditions for organic life are present. This number, says Shapley, "is a minimum and personally I would recommend . . . its multiplication by at least a thousand times, possibly by a million."[3]

It can be argued, of course, that this is just speculation; but it is speculation by a highly respected astronomer and cosmologist, after a lifetime of scientific discipline. Other astronomers may question his figures concerning the frequency of extraterrestrial life, but few would deny that his conclusion is probably correct. And this conclusion is not only that life arose naturally on this utterly undistinguished planet of a common star; but also that "at least one star in a billion will have with it a crusted nongaseous planet entirely suitable for living organisms."[4]

If, then, there are at least a hundred million life-sustaining earths, is there any remote likelihood that we human beings are unique, or that we stand at the biological, moral, intellectual

(3) *Ibid.*, p. 74.
(4) *Ibid.*, p. 77.

and spiritual apex of living creatures? If our sun is average, our stellar associations ordinary and our location in space in no way special, is there any reason not to suppose that, on at least some of these millions of other earths, the evolutionary process has carried life far beyond anything we even can imagine?

All this is a blow — a salutary one, I think — to our human vanity. For it is hard enough to think of our solar system as far out on the fringe of the Milky Way. It is still harder to absorb the fact that our galaxy is but one of millions of galaxies. And it is hardest of all to admit that, in all probability, far higher forms of life than ours exist on at least a million other warm, moist, star-lit planets.

Tragically, we have not yet become citizens of the world, let alone the Milky Way. We have not yet overcome our tribal provincialisms, our racial prejudices, our nationalistic chauvinism. Perhaps recognition of the cosmic immensities and our relative insignificance in the vast scheme of things will encourage us to outgrow our provincialism and prejudice and suicidal national rivalries. Perhaps, if we went out more often to ponder beneath the stars and to read their messages (as interpreted by modern science), we would be readier to reach out to take our brother's hand, whether his skin or his language matched ours or not.

We have spoken of man and of space, but only in passing of the third word in our topic: "God." Can we humans move out to claim our cosmic citizenship and not lose God entirely? I add the word "entirely," because I think we have pretty nearly lost Him already. I don't just mean Unitarians, either. The orthodox may quip that when and if Unitarians pray, they pray "to whom it may concern." But I suspect theirs will not be the last laugh. The supernatural Deity of orthodox religion is dead, and has been dead, as Nietzsche knew, for quite some time. The Deus ex Machina, the Creator-God outside this exploding cosmos of a thousand million galaxies, is no longer a particularly meaningful hypothesis.

What is not dead, as Nietzsche also knew, is the hunger for God — the hunger that caused him to write:

Yea, I will know Thee, great Unknown,
Who shakest the foundations of my soul,
Urgent and clamorous as the thunder's roll,
Eternally apart, eternally my own,
Yea, I will know Thee — I will serve Thee.

Because men hunger for God, they cling to their idols; and if we have human understanding, we do not ridicule this clinging. We also know this hunger and the tragedy of what Martin Buber graphically calls "the eclipse of God." But we shall not recover God by roaming through space, or by clinging to a pre-scientific belief in a supernatural cosmic monarch. This is a concept which, as we orient ourselves to the new vision of our universe, we must jettison, along with our human vanity and anthropocentric provincialism.

But though God as an independent, supernatural, miracle-working Being is dead — or at least has vanished beyond the fleeing galaxies — what Nietzsche called "the great Unknown, who shakest the foundations of my soul" remains. The way to personal, intimate communion with the ultimate reality in which we live and move and have our being is as open to us as to our ancestors.

We cannot find God in this terrifying vastness by training our mightiest telescopes on distant galaxies. Rather, let us abandon all notion of Him as a Being like ourselves, a "Man writ large." Let us abandon all preconceived ideas, all inherited anthropomorphic images. Let us turn inward, school our spirits in tranquillity and train our inner vision. Thus, as Wordsworth put it:

With an eye made quiet by the power
Of Harmony, and the deep power of joy,
We see into the life of things.

I hold no special brief for the word "God"; confusing and overburdened as it is, I simply find it the least inadequate word we have, as we grope after the added dimension of life, beyond space and time, matter and energy.

"O how may I ever express that secret word?" sang the fif-
teenth-century Indian poet and saint, Kabir.

O, how can I say: He is not like this, He is like that?
If I say He is within me, the universe is shamed.
If I say He is without me, that is false.
He makes the inner and the outer world to be indivisibly one;
The conscious and the unconscious both are his footstools.
He is neither manifest nor hidden:
He is neither revealed nor unrevealed.
There are no words to tell what He is.

These are, of course, the words of an oriental mystic, and mysti-
cism has long been suspect in the West. We have so concentrated
our attention on the mastery of external nature as to become
virtual strangers to ourselves. Our Western religion has sought
to authenticate itself by miracle and supernatural revelation,
supported by an elaborate ritual and by infallible dogma. But
now these supports melt away.

If we are to recover God, we had best learn from those who
have known Him in their own personal experience. And learn
also from those who, like Kabir, happily phrased their thoughts
about God without setting forth a supernatural concept that flies
in the face of scientific theories. Such men point a way — I suspect, the only way — that is open to us, if we are to know Him
in Whom alone our restless hearts can find peace.

So it is that I call you to cosmic citizenship and to a more
inward life. I call upon you to roam the heavens, to "range
through all their length and breadth, their height and depth,
past, present and to come" — an earthbound provincial no
longer. I call upon you to roam that universe that you yourself
are, learning anew what we have found so easy to forget — that
"our true life lies at a great depth within us." "You can never,"
said Heraclitus, "find the boundaries of the soul, so deep are
they." And no one has ever yet contradicted him.

Harlow Shapley is right: we cannot hope to know the truth
about our world, or weigh aright our human significance, unless
we courageously follow the scientists' explorations of space and

time and energy and matter. This is an essential corrective to our vanity and egocentrism.

But hymn-writer Hosmer was also right. God is not to be found "in far-off realms of space." He is rather to be sought within ourselves, through cultivation of a more contemplative and more spacious inner life.

Quenching the Fires of Hell

by *Arthur Foote*

For well over a century, Unitarians have generally recognized their close affinity to the loosely knit, decentralized, liberal religious movement known as Universalism. Universalists, on their part, have generally known themselves to be theological next of kin to us. The present proposal looking to the organic merger of these sister movements, therefore, contains no element of surprise. Indeed, many people, for many years, have wondered why these two have not become one. I suspect that the reason is more cultural than theological.

In the first place, Universalists, like Unitarians, have tended to be an extremely individualistic bunch. Many of them have been "come-outers" from restrictive, narrow, creedal churches. They were interested in the freedom of the Universalist movement, in its rational interpretation of life, of the Bible and of Christian doctrine. They were disinclined to take concerted action to build a new denomination. As one historian notes: "Its adherents were not promoters or organizers; their dominant interest was not building churches. They were suspicious of the encroachments of ecclesiasticism upon individual freedom."[1]

Both movements have suffered institutionally from this reluctance of their members to commit themselves to any form of organization. Both failed to capitalize on their opportunity for great growth as the frontier moved westward. The Universalists particularly were rather ardent missionaries. But, distrusting institutionalism, they considered themselves as liberalizers, liberators, rather than as builders of a new denomination.

Historically, neither group has been sectarian in spirit or primarily interested in institutional growth. Having been less guilty than most Protestant churches of the shameful, divisive,

---

(1) Clinton L. Scott, *A Short History of Universalism*, Boston, Universalist Publishing House, 1957, p. 12.

competitive sectarian spirit, we are perhaps less strongly motivated toward church union than many others.

But when I say that the barrier to merger has been cultural
rather than theological, I mean more than this individualism
and this distrust of institutionalism. Unitarianism has been
characterized from the beginning, by outsiders, as a movement of
"the intellectual elite." Its membership has included a dispro-
portionally large number of the nation's leaders — in politics,
education, science, literature and social reform. Astonishingly,
twenty-one of the eighty-six busts in the Hall of Fame are of
members of this numerically tiny movement.

Little credit attaches to us, it seems to me, for this fact that
so many prominent persons have claimed Unitarian affiliation.
Just as we ought to reject the idea of guilt by association, so we
should reject the idea of virtue by association. A more valid
point is that Unitarianism has been an upper-middle class movement, appealing largely to college graduates and professional
people — not to the socially elite or the extremely wealthy, but
to the intelligentsia; a movement predominantly urban, whose
churches usually survive in the smaller communities only when
they are college towns.

Universalism, by contrast, has been a middle to lower-middle
class movement. It has never made deep inroads among the
intellectually elite, but has been a predominantly rural movement, drawing its membership from farmers, artisans, tradesmen
and workers. Until the 1880s its ministry was, like the Methodist,
untrained, lacking not only in graduate school but even in college education. Even today, many of its older ministers lack
theological degrees. Nowadays, the theological students of both
churches go to the same schools and receive the same education,
but many of the intellectually more able graduates still tend
toward the Unitarian ministry.

There has always been free movement back and forth between these two ministries; and this has generally worked to the
disadvantage of the Universalists. Unitarian churches, being
more urban and somewhat larger and wealthier, have generally

offered better salaries and higher professional prestige. The result has been a kind of siphoning off of the cream of the Universalist ministry. That has been one of the main reasons, I suspect,
why Universalism has not shown the growth in recent decades
which Unitarianism has experienced.

Another reason for this lack of growth, obviously, has been
the rural nature of Universalism. This has not been an era when
village and crossroads churches have prospered.

Now, when you combine the extremely individualistic, anti-
ecclesiastical character of both groups, and this pronounced cultural difference between them, you can see why a Universalist-
Unitarian marriage was not consummated long ago and why it
still remains (however desirable theoretically) a difficult and, in
the eyes of some, even a hazardous venture.

I have no desire to hide from you where I stand on merger.
To do so, in fact, would be to evade my duty as your minister.
I am for it, as I have been for more than twenty years. Soon
after I came to St. Paul, Carl Olson of the Minneapolis Universalist Church asked me why I had never become a Universalist
minister, as well as a Unitarian. Finding no good answer, I
applied for and was granted such status. (Today, some twenty
per cent of our Unitarian ministers have this dual fellowship.)

This would seem to commit me to being promerger, but
being a liberal entails a willingness to re-examine one's own
position whenever challenged to do so. I have, in recent months,
reopened the whole idea, eagerly reading every antimerger argument and talking with anyone I could find opposed to merger.
The result has been a more sober realization of the practical difficulties that will have to be solved, but a continued conviction
that America needs a united liberal church, that there are no
morally sound arguments for opposing merger and that both
movements need each other. Universalism needs our greater intellectual vigor; and we need its broader cultural base, its more
folksy approach, its ability to set forth the liberal gospel in terms
more appealing and understandable to the so-called common
man.

This question of uniting our two denominations is a decision fraught with large implications for the future of religious liberalism in America. One of the first things to help us understand whether merger is wise is, I think, a little more historical background.

Historically defined, Universalism is the doctrine that it is the purpose of God, as revealed through Christ, to save every member of the human family from sin and damnation. Universalists, narrowly defined, are simply people who don't believe in hell. They believe "that the ethical character of God is such that it is His will to bring the entire human race into a state of holiness and happiness."

In this sense, Universalism is very ancient. Clement of Alexandria, in the second century, the first great scholar of the Christian church, taught universal salvation, as did Origen, "the first Christian liberal." Not until 544, under Emperor Justinian, was belief in universal salvation condemned as heresy.

Despite the condemnation of the church and vigorous efforts to crush this "heresy," it persisted through to the Protestant Reformation among brave individuals, such as Joannes Scotus Erigena, who boldly declared that God's all-loving nature is incompatible with eternal punishment, and among such heretical sects as the Lollards and the mystical Brethren of the Common Life. After the Reformation, Luther and Calvin joined the Roman inquisition against this "heresy" of God's goodness and man's ultimate salvation. Many of the groups loosely lumped together as Anabaptists preached universal salvation as one of their radical doctrines.

When immigration to America became possible toward the end of the seventeenth century, these persecuted Protestant dissenters flocked to the New World — particularly to Pennsylvania, where religious toleration prevailed. Among these were Huguenots, Dunkers, Moravians, Mennonites and Schwenkfelders. These were people broadly characterized as Pietists, groups stressing religion as a way of living rather than as conformity to creed. They took their Bible study seriously and sought to follow literally in the steps of Jesus.

Among these Pietists was the man sometimes called "the Father of American Universalism," George de Benneville. As a lad of seventeen, de Benneville was imprisoned in France for preaching universal salvation and was sentenced to be beheaded. Saved by a last-minute reprieve, he became an itinerant preacher in Germany, Holland, Belgium and Italy. His ministry was spiced by occasional periods of incarceration. Eventually he came to Pennsylvania, in 1741, when he was still only thirty-eight years old. Here, as a physician and lay preacher, he continued to travel and spread his gospel for more than fifty years, finding his message eagerly received by many of the various dissenting groups. De Benneville founded no churches; he was content to sow the seeds of a more humane gospel — seeds from which grew the Universalist Church of America.

Religious ferment and a continuance of the Protestant Reformation was not confined to Pennsylvania. Up in New England during the same century, the groundwork for Unitarianism was being laid. Within the Calvinist churches — the tax-supported established church — the liberal spirit was steadily spreading. The harsher doctrines of Calvinism were being quietly laid to rest.

It is not strange, therefore, to learn that Universalism gained a foothold in Massachusetts about the time of the American Revolution. It was in the sea-faring town of Gloucester, whose ships sailed the seven seas and brought home all sorts of cargo, including strange ideas and heretical books, that the first Universalist church was established. Its founder was one John Murray, an Englishman born in 1741, the year de Benneville came to America. He was the son of strict Calvinists, who impressed upon him, as he later wrote, "a terror of religion." His father seldom even indulged in a smile and taught him "that for anyone, not the elect of God, to say of God . . . 'Our Father,' was nothing better than blasphemy." As a young man, hearing the fervid preaching of John Wesley, he became a Methodist, but was shortly excommunicated for questioning the doctrine that only the elect would be saved. This experience, coupled with the death of his young wife, left him downhearted and dejected. Resolving, as he put it, to "close my days in solitude, in the most complete retirement," he set sail for America.

But life had other plans in store for him. Landing in New Jersey, he was befriended by a Universalist family who prevailed upon him to preach. His eloquence and his emphasis upon the love of God and the promise of universal salvation met favorable response. Within a few years, he became the minister of a little group of Gloucester Universalists. With them, in 1779, he founded the first Universalist church in America.

Murray was still largely a Calvinist: he rejected only the doctrine of eternal punishment, according to which only the elect are predestined to salvation. It has been said of him that "he widened predestination to include all mankind." But the theology of John Murray seems far removed from modern Universalism. The fires of hell have long been quenched, and it requires considerable imagination to put ourselves in the place of our forebears who were so deeply preoccupied with the issue of soul-salvation.

This history is interesting chiefly for the light it throws on Universalism. Theologically as well as culturally, Universalism sprang from very different seed than Unitarianism. Our movement was a vigorous intellectual protest against all the major doctrines of Calvinism. Its spokesmen included many of the best educated men in New England. Channing, in his famous Baltimore Sermon, took all the principal tenets of Calvin, repudiated them and affirmed the positive opposing principles — the goodness of God, the thorough-going humanity of Jesus, the moral dignity of human nature, the validity of reason and the duty of free inquiry.

One of the many Universalist ministers to become Unitarian was Thomas Starr King. Minister of the First Unitarian Church of San Francisco at the beginning of the Civil War, King stumped the state pleading against secession, and was credited with "saving California for the Union." His bust is in the Hall of Fame. Asked to explain the difference between the two denominations, he quipped: "Universalists believe that God is too good to damn them; and Unitarians believe they are too good to be damned."

Like many such sayings, Starr King's words carry much truth. Unitarians usually have been anti-Trinitarians; but their central doctrine has been the dignity and perfectability of man. And Universalism has been, before all else, a movement affirming the goodness, the love of God.

The Unitarian repudiation of Calvinism was intellectual and thoroughgoing. The Universalists were content, in the beginning, with a simpler, emotional rejection of the idea of God as Calvin portrayed him. As such, Universalism made wide appeal to thousands of simple, unlettered folk — folk who had known the torments, not of hell itself, but of the fear of hell. Folk like Caleb Rich, who wrote: "I often looked upon the insects and poisonous reptiles, thinking how much better their lot was in this world than mine."

We cannot conclude this thumbnail sketch of early Universalism without brief mention of the greatest name in Universalist history, that of Hosea Ballou. Ballou was the son of a Baptist minister in New Hampshire. His schooling was limited; "his face was bronzed by work in the fields, his arm strengthened by hard labor with axe and scythe, his eye clear from daily contact with hills and mountains, and his mind fired by an independent, patient study of the Bible."[2] Not only an eloquent preacher, Ballou thought his own way out of Calvinism, rejecting the idea that some are saved and others damned, that God hates this depraved and lost world, that Jesus' death appeased God's wrath and that Jesus and God are coequal in that mysterious something called the Trinity.

When still in his early thirties, he wrote a remarkable book — *A Treatise on the Atonement*, published in 1805 — which proved pivotal in Universalist theology. More than a decade before Channing's great sermon in Baltimore, it frankly set forth the Unitarian theological position. Jesus' death, Ballou reasoned, was not to reconcile God to man, but rather man to God. It has

---

(2) Alfred S. Cole, *Our Liberal Heritage,* Beacon Reference Series, Boston, Beacon Press, 1951, p. 21.

been stated that less than ten years after Ballou's book appeared, only two Universalist preachers still held trinitarian views. This surely is an exaggeration; but with Hosea Ballou, Universalist theology turned the corner that has brought it steadily closer to Unitarianism.

The crucial fact is that Universalism, like Unitarianism, escaped being strait-jacketed into a creed. With few exceptions, it has admirably maintained the right of individual opinion and adhered to Ballou's words: "If we agree in brotherly love, there is no disagreement that can do us any injury; but if we do not, no other agreement can do us any good." At various conventions, declarations of faith have been drawn up; but they have never been made obligatory or binding on individuals or churches.

From the time of Ballou onward, Universalism, like Unitarianism, has moved towards the free use of reason and reliance upon scientific methods in the discovery of truths. As the fires of hell died down, Universalism found universal salvation an inadequate gospel; its assertion of the love of God lost its uniqueness. Many other churches "subdued their emphasis upon damnation." If this was all the gospel Universalism had to proclaim, its mission had been accomplished. But its present-day leaders maintain otherwise. In the words of Carl H. Olson:

Originally dealing with one "universal" — that of salvation — our faith has grown to include others. Today, Universalism stands for assertion of the universal value of religion, regardless of its name or background. Universalists assert that the voice of God has sounded in many lands and that all religions, in their best forms, reflect a similar message and inspiration. We stand for the Universal Fatherhood of God, believing that no single race or creedal group has a monopoly of favor. We stand for the Universal Brotherhood of Man, and for the obligation of all to work toward universal justice, harmony and love.[3]

In short, Universalism, in the eyes of its ablest exponents, is one-worldism in religion — a religious movement placing the

_____
(3) From a sermon, "New Reasons for Old Rules."

emphasis squarely on freedom of belief, on the supreme worth of human personality, on faith in mankind and in universal values. The salvation it offers our age is not simply salvation from the fires of hell — fires quite adequately quenched — but rather salvation as "the process of bringing persons to the full realization of their potential greatness — extended to all mankind."

The Last Event and Its Picture of God

by George G. Brooks

Easter speaks of immortality, but it gives silent testimony to much more — if we are to listen to Christian theology. Immortality is a possible and honorable *faith,* but we cannot consent to the other implications of Easter without a deep affront to our moral nature.

With us, belief in immortality is a personal choice. We can believe it to be true, or we can strongly deny it, or we can stay agnostically neutral. We know there is no real evidence one way or the other; no one has returned from the after-life, and no one knows enough to say dogmatically that something of a person cannot be preserved in some fashion after death. The rationalists, finding no good evidence for belief, reject immortality out of hand as a wish-projection, as indeed it initially is. The romanticists, with no evidence for nonbelief and finding a buoyancy to life by holding the belief, assert, beyond and in spite of no evidence, that the after-life is a truth. Either assertion is faith without evidence: this is what faith is.

I for one cannot be dogmatic for either position. I hold to a conditional and open-ended faith — that *if* there is an after-life, it is the same for all people, and it is not to be feared. For these two elements of faith — the universality (or sameness) of immortality, if it exists, and its unfearsome nature, if it exists — I know there is no evidence. But it makes me certain in my own mind that, no matter what I think or do, I cannot alter what will happen to me — or to any part of me that might transcend death and thus I need not be anxious in this life concerning my future life. This might be fatalism, but I believe it is wiser in this area not to be presumptuous.

I live very happily with this conditional faith, knowing full well that, if there is no after-life, these same things are true. Moreover, the less complex and anxiety-producing my beliefs are in this area, the more and fuller attention I can give to thoughts that relate to living in the present world. So my faith is a conditional, agnostic faith, having in it no room for fear or anxiety. I like to feel that it is closely allied to the historic Universalist faith that rejected hell and made salvation for all men an integral part of its theology.

When I turn, however, to the Easter story and Christian theology as they relate to Jesus' death and resurrection, I become troubled. For faith in immortality is made dogmatic, and the proof for this dogma is made to rest on what mankind knows to be a pseudohistorical document, the New Testament, which Christians themselves admit is more a testament of faith than a document of fact. Their "evidence" is acknowledged to be a mixture of fact and fancy, yet they preach their belief as if it were certain truth. Any person may believe in immortality, even without evidence, but it is the better part of judgment to recognize the character of this faith and not become dogmatic in its exposition.

But what disturbs me most in the Easter celebration is the picture of God that must be accepted to make the death and resurrection theologically airtight. This is typified by a 1958 Lenten editorial of the nondenominational *Christian Century*. This is a fairly liberal, middle-of-the-road Christian journal of wide circulation, and the author of the editorial was the dean of a highly respected, nonfanatical but deeply Christian-oriented divinity school. So the point of view can with fairness be taken as representative of Christian thinking.

"Who was responsible for the death of Jesus?" asked the author. After pointing out the many who might be held responsible (such as the Temple authorities, Judas, Pilate and the Roman magistrates, with their concern for order), he answers:

Jesus was not delivered up by his generation alone. He was delivered "according to the definite plan and foreknowledge of God." [Acts 2:23] The events of Good Friday have more behind them than the ignorance or fanaticism or weakness of the particular persons involved in them. God was at work. "God was in Christ reconciling the world to himself." [II Cor. 5:19] Who

was then responsible? . . . In the last analysis God was the responsible one, since God so purposed and accomplished the
redemption of man.

The Easter story, in Christian eyes, is inexorably tied to the
theory of redemption and the working of God to bring this about.
This being so, the fall of Adam and man's loss of a sinless nature
(and with it, eternal life) cannot be divorced from any theology
of Easter. Jesus' death would have no exceptional meaning were
it not as a redemption for man's sin. This is the meaning of
Jesus as one's Savior — and the word has no other meaning.
We cannot escape the Garden of Eden when we look at the hill
of Calvary. In Christian theology, Jesus' death effected this redemption from sin because Jesus was not a man but God's son,
the second figure of the Trinity. Only such a death was a suitable
atonement for man's sin.

Now, what picture of God does this give us? First of all, it
shows God as a very primitive man, with no finer instincts than
a primitive man. For we know that primitive man, in order to
atone for his mistakes or to get on the good side of Deity, sacri-
ficed his son as a blood offering. Is there any difference between
this and "God . . . gave his only begotten Son"? [John 3:16]
Yet if any man today should sacrifice his child on an altar to
effect some reconciliation with God, he would be put either in a
mental hospital or on the electric chair. For men have become
morally sensitive to such an action. To this extent, at least, we
are no longer primitive.

Easter, it seems to me, asks us to worship 'a God Whose
moral sense is less than our own. I think it is moral blindness
when Christian worshipers are unable to see this. I think it is
hypocrisy when Christian writers try to explain it away by
rationalizations, or to conceal it under an aura of sacrificial love.

Take another example: with the sin of Adam (which is in-
escapably tied up with Easter), Christian theology says that man
both loses eternal life and gains an everlasting sinful nature.
As Rev. Berkeley Blake has pointed out, this is the original
formulation of the doctrine of massive retaliation. The sin of

the father is visited, not just on the father, but on the sons, grandsons, granddaughters and every future generation ever to live — the innocent as well as the guilty.

For most of us, however, the idea of punishing a man's children or descendants for the man's crime contravenes our elementary sense of justice. Yet the God of Easter theology is guilty of the ultimate in this travesty of justice. What kind of moral sensitivity do we have if we worship Him? (Perhaps it was no accident that the author of the modern doctrine of massive retaliation was the son of a Christian minister. For if you can accept God as the punisher of all men for the crime of one, you can accept more easily a policy that would kill the innocent with the guilty.

Easter theology is, in short, self-defeating. It deadens our moral nature and leads us to accept *any* picture of God if only it proves that Jesus' death and resurrection guarantees us life after death and grace from sin.

If we are morally sensitive, our quarrel should be with what Easter has done to God, regardless of what it might indicate for men. Our concern should be with the moral nature of the God men are asked to worship, and what happens to men when the morality of their God is less than their own. We must strive to make our God-concept, the object of our worship and reverence, worthy of our own highest moral ideals and a challenge for us to emulate. To do less is to remain chained to our infancy. To meet the challenge is to make our religion relevant to our growth in moral understanding.

Religion's Worst Enemy

by Herbert F. Vetter, Jr.

In Martin Luther's battle hymn of the Reformation are these words of fighting faith:

> Still our ancient foe
> Doth seek to work us woe.
> His craft and power are great;
> And, armed with cruel hate,
> On earth is not his equal.

The words are strange with power. But what is, who is this ancient foe? Who is this enemy of faith? What is the worst enemy of religion in the modern world?

Is the worst enemy of religion pride? Is it that haughty, classic weasel in the soul, renowned for thriving on and driving toward destruction by tearing down others' personalities so that one's own self-esteem may be exalted to new heights? Is it pride of intellect? pride of property, such as the home in which one lives? pride of family, whether ancestral or contemporary? pride of position, or occupation, of status in the community?

Or is the worst enemy of religion selfishness, the selfishness from which this spirit of arrogance flows? Is it the selfishness that would center all life in one's own person, regardless of the cost to other people — the selfishness that is the untamed fountain of anger and hatred, envy and lust for power, falsehood and greed? Is that the worst enemy of religion?

Or is the enemy of enemies not so much personal as social? Is the worst enemy of religion today nationalism — that passionate attachment to one's own country which blinds one to the needs and hopes of other nations? Is it that idolatrous devotion to one's native land whch now deadlocks the world in parochial strife?

Or is it racism — that radical denial of the brotherhood of man which again and again erupts to plague the conscience of

150

modern man, dividing mankind according to the ridiculous standard of skin pigment?

Or is it modern war, that puncturer of our pretense to love — the modern war of total populations, by total populations, against total populations? Is total war, war for total stakes, the worst enemy of religion?

As I have reflected on this question, I have been driven toward the conclusion that the worst enemy of religion is not any of these particular personal or social evils, but something which is at once more ultimate and more inclusive — the source from which pride, selfishness, nationalism, racism and war forever grow. I suggest that the worst enemy of religion is religion. As so often happens, the corruption of the best yields the worst. It is not without reason, then, that Paul Tillich, the most creative systematic theologian currently at work in America, has declared: "The first word of religion is the word against religion." One might well add that the first word of theology is the word against theology.

This thesis, that the worst enemy of religion is religion, swings sharply counter to the main currents of our time, for today religion is all too effectively exempt from criticism. "You must have faith!" we are repeatedly told, as if faith in faith were sufficient to redeem us from destruction. In view of the contemporary resurgence of religious interest, it is particularly important that certain questions be posed — and answered — without evasion, questions about contemporary religion:

What is the most segregated hour of the week? Eleven A.M. *each Sunday morning.*

On which area of the earth has more blood been shed than anywhere else? The Holy Land.

What institution in the modern world most rigidly adheres to irrelevant patterns of the past? The church.

What branch of modern knowledge is most provincial in its basic attitudes and assumptions? I fear it is my own branch, theology.

What aspect of our culture has contributed the most to un-

realistic ethics and the irresponsibility of other worldliness?
Religion.

In the face of such questions and their all too painful answers, can we defend religion's exemption from criticism? Prophetic religion ever must say *No!*

The first word of religion is indeed the word against religion. For example, if you think of religion as a pure fountainhead of toleration and goodwill, you may be challenged by this letter written by a distinguished American in 1682:

To ye Aged and Beloved Mr. John Higginson:
    There be now at sea a ship called Welcome which has on board 100 or more heretics and malignants called Quakers, with Mr. Penn, who is a scamp at the head of them. The General Court has accordingly given sacred orders to Master Malachi Bascott of the brig Porpoise to waylay said Welcome slyly as near the Cape of Cod as may be, and make captive of the same Penn and his ungodly crew, so that the Lord may be glorified and not mocked on the soil of this new country with the heathen worship of these people. Much spoil can be made selling the whold lot to Barbadoes where slaves fetch good prices in rum and sugar, and we shall not only do the Lord great good by punishing the wicked, but we shall make great good for the minister and his people.
Yours in the bowels of Christ,
Cotton Mather

Has not religion a responsibility to speak the word against its enemy of enemies, religion? Would you wish to exempt the fanatical faith of Cotton Mather from the discipline of criticism?

There is more, ever more documentary evidence before us, even in the Bible itself. In the Old Testament, the height of ethical religion was attained by the prophets, who sent the thrust of their attacks against the false religion of their day. Listen to the words of Isaiah:

    What to me is the multitude of your sacrifices? says the Lord. . . . Bring no more vain offerings. . . . I cannot endure iniquity and solemn assembly. Your new moons and your appointed feasts my soul hates; they have become a burden to me, I am weary of bearing them. When you spread forth your hands, I will hide my eyes from you; even though you make many prayers, I will not listen; your hands are full of blood. [Isaiah 1:11-15; RSV]

Consider the life and teachings of Jesus of Nazareth, who stood heroically in the line of the Hebrew prophets. Were not his harshest words spoken against the religious leaders of his own day? One of his disciples left us this invigorating record of a decisive event and address:

While he was speaking, a Pharisee asked him to dine with him; so he went in and sat at the table. The Pharisee was astonished to see that he did not first wash before dinner. And the Lord said to him, "Now you Pharisees cleanse the outside of the cup and of the dish, but inside you are full of extortion and wickedness. You fools! Did not he who made the outside make the inside also? But give for alms those things which are within; and behold, everything is clean for you.

"But woe to you Pharisees! for you tithe mint and rue and every herb, and neglect justice and the love of God; these you ought to have done, without neglecting the others. Woe to you Pharisees! for you love the best seat in the synagogues and salutations in the market places. Woe to you! for you are like graves which are not seen, and men walk over them without knowing it." [Luke 11:37-44; RSV]

Prophetic religion, in contrast to the religion of mere amiability, has ever in diverse ways cried out: "Beware of the clergy!" My own first word as one who seeks to live a religious life must ever be a word against religion's worst enemy, religion. My first word as a clergyman must be a word against the clergy, of which I am one.

When Billy Graham brought his crusade of archaic fundamentalism into New York City, the Protestant clergy of almost all denominations, large and small, joined the bandwagon to support his cause. Protestant clergy of all persuasions graced the platform of piety. Radical questions about the validity of Graham's streamlined yet old-fashioned revivalism were deemed out of order. In America's major metropolis, the Protestant clergy closed ranks in a crusade whose victory, said *The Christian Century,* a vigorous, nondenominational Protestant weekly, would set American religion back more than fifty years. Apart from Reinhold Niebuhr and the *Century,* one could find very few outspoken, independent critics of the Graham crusade.

This situation was not atypical. *Be positive, eternally positive,* say the clergy and the people. How many Americans have ever heard a sermon which spoke in praise of doubt? An all too common maxim of the clergy is: leave your doubts in the study when you enter the pulpit. As if their hearers could not bear to hear the truth! As if the congregation needed to take refuge in traditional illusions — in a lazy, meandering faith which refuses to grapple with the doubts of modern man. Across the pulpits of America three words are written in a bloodless, invisible ink: PROPHETS NOT WANTED.

Some years ago, Thomas Jefferson noted the lethargy of the clergy in moving beyond the status quo toward an actual democracy. On the basis of his experience and observation, he concluded that "the clergy, by getting themselves established by law and engrafted into the machine of government, have been a very formidable engine against the civil and religious rights of man." Alexander Hamilton wrote, with reference to the established churches: "What influences in fact have ecclesiastical establishments had on Civil Society? In some instances they have been seen to erect a spiritual tyranny on the ruins of Civil Authority: in many instances they have been seen upholding the thrones of political tyranny; in no instance have they been seen the guardians of the liberties of the people."

Almost alone among the churches, the Unitarian heritage has not brimmed with affirmation devoid of the critical temper. Without a full and freely flowing measure of the courage to doubt, the liberal movement in religion would never have sprung into being. As heirs of the protestant spirit, we have kept the edge of rational and prophetic criticism carefully honed. Although the burning stake was his lot, Michael Servetus was not afraid to declare his honest doubts. In writing *On the Errors of the Trinity,* he observed:

How much this tradition of the Trinity has, alas! been a laughing-stock to the Mohammedans, only God knows. The Jews also shrink from giving adherence to this fancy of ours, and laugh at our foolishness about the Trinity . . . And not only Mohammedans and Hebrews, but the very beasts of the field, would make fun of us did they grasp our fantastical notion, for all the world of the Lord bless the one God.

If we turn to the most notable champions of the Unitarian outlook in this country, we find the same awareness of faith's deep demand for doubt. William Ellery Channing, in his discourse on "Spiritual Freedom," gave ample recognition of the positive power of religion, interpreting it as "the mightiest agent in human affairs," to which "belongs pre-eminently the work of freeing and elevating the mind." At the same time, Channing noted that:

Intolerance always shelters itself under the name and garb of religious zeal. . . . Let religion be seized on by individuals or sects, as their special province; let them clothe themselves with God's prerogative of judgment; let them succeed in enforcing their creed by penalties of law or penalties of opinion; let them succeed in fixing a brand on virtuous men, whose only crime is free investigation; and religion becomes the most blighting tyranny which can establish itself over the mind.

The worst enemy of religion is religion, and an obligation is laid upon us to meet and to rout this enemy. How can this be done?

The first obligation of free men is to exercise the courage to doubt. Here is strange doctrine indeed! Religion, our churches tell us, is defense of faith. I would suggest, however, that doubt is faith's hidden affirmation. The men of noblest faith have been men of strongest doubt. Out of Gautama's doubts about the prevailing Hinduism of his day has sprung one of our major world faiths, Buddhism. Out of the doubts of Socrates emerged the vital intellectual force of Western civilization. Out of the doubts of Jesus about the established religion of his day came both his crucifixion and the Christian faith. Out of the doubts of Luther arose Protestantism's fighting faith. Out of the doubts of Freud and Neitzsche, Kierkegaard and Whitehead is coming now a New Reformation in religion, a New Reformation open to the demands of world civilization. Forever out of doubt grows faith.

In such a setting, then, we need not only the classic emphasis of the Epistle of James concerning faith and works; we need also a new fusion — of faith and doubt. Modern man's will to believe is twisted out of shape unless it is tempered by the courage to doubt. Doubt is the modern citadel of freedom, standing in eternal opposition to tyranny's idols of infallibility. Courage to doubt is free faith's vital center. Whosoever would be a man must be a doubter. Encounter with doubt is eternally the price of honest faith. Whoever would ascend to the heights of creative living must first pass through the valley of the shadow of doubt. Capacity for doubt is a measure of manhood. Ability to doubt is one of the surest guarantees of mature faith.

Out of modern man's doubt concerning sacred idols of infallibility arose his faith in individual freedom of belief as the living center of a responsibly concerned community.

Out of modern man's doubt concerning walls which thwart the growth of life — walls of national prejudice and pride, of religious exclusiveness, of racial arrogance, of vindictive caste and class — emerged his stand for unrestricted use of reason in religion as the guiding, discipling agent of faith that makes men free and whole, members one of another in a world community of life.

Out of modern man's doubt concerning every form of tyranny over the mind and body, heart and soul of man has come his faith in generous tolerance of differing religious views and practices within a context of commitment to the democratic process in church and state, school and industry and home.

Out of modern man's doubt concerning the superstitions, bigotry and idolatry of particular churches comes now his growing faith in the Church Universal, uniting people of diverse faiths everywhere in sacred common quest of "truth for the mind; good works for the hands; love for the heart; and for the soul, that aspiring after perfection . . . which, like lightning in the clouds, shines brightest when elsewhere it is most dark."[1]

The courage to doubt is the nerve of freedom and of freedom's faith. The courage to doubt is, paradoxically, the hope of the Church Universal, for wisdom of doubt is a prelude to faith. The courage to doubt is eternally essential if the church is not to surrender to barbarism but is to serve the Kingdom of God with undiluted strength of heart and hand, mind and soul. In our warfare against religion's worst enemy — the enemy who incorporates the life-destroying forces of pride, selfishness, nationalism, war, racism and tyranny — we deeply need the courage to doubt. Only thus can our faith be manifest with powerful relevance in the modern world.

---

(1) Theodore Parker, "The True Idea of a Christian Church," *The Collected Works of Theodore Parker*, London, Trübner & Co., 1875, Vol. III, p. 54.

The Commitment
Practical Religion

The only religion is conscience in action.

HENRY DEMAREST LLOYD

Notes on Contributors

Edward A. Cahill is minister of the United Liberal Church in Atlanta, Georgia.

Alfred McClung Lee is a graduate professor of sociology and anthropology at Brooklyn College in Brooklyn, New York, and a member of the Garden City Unitarian Fellowship.

Jack Mendelsohn is minister of the Arlington Street Church in Boston, Massachusetts.

William H. Odell is a vice president of International Harvester Company, Chicago, and a member of the North Shore Unitarian Church in Deerfield, Illinois.

Curtis W. Reese, retired, was executive director of the Western Unitarian Conference and dean of the Abraham Lincoln Centre in Chicago.

Philip Schug is regional director of the Southwestern Unitarian Conference and minister of the First Unitarian Church in San Antonio, Texas.

Alvah W. Sulloway, a lawyer in Darien, Connecticut, is the author of *Birth Control and Catholic Doctrine,* published by the Beacon Press in 1959.

The Function of a Modern Minister

by Curtis W. Reese

The ministry is an ancient and honorable profession. It is related to the basic needs of human nature and should be regarded as a permanent institution in the life of man. No other profession deals more basically or intimately with the human situation. The ministry, therefore, is a profession, the practice of which should be approached with the most adequate preparation, the most enlightened skills and the greatest possible devotion. Nothing less than the fullest commitment, the greatest possible store of appropriate knowledge and the most refined skills should be the equipment of the modern minister as he tackles the multitudinous functions of his profession.

Let me outline what appear to me to be the functions of the modern minister in the major fields with which he is concerned.

The first function of the modern minister is to embody in his own life the ethical ideals and the high excellence for which religion and the profession of the ministry stand. Failure in this respect in relation to family, friends, associates or neighbors is failure of the first order. Honesty, truthfulness and integrity are basic equipment for the minister, as are generosity of spirit, graciousness of manner and dependable behavior. The minister as a family man, as a churchman and as a citizen simply must be above reproach. He must be thoughtful and considerate in all his relationships. He must be calm in temper, generous in attitude and gentlemanly in all ways. There can be no excuse for a minister who is dilatory, careless or slippery in his conduct. Underhanded dealing and lack of openness are sins that cannot be tolerated in the life of a minister. He stands before his congregation and the community as an exemplar of excellence in thought and life, and he must not lower himself, profane his profession and betray religion by living unworthily of his high calling.

All, absolutely all, of the other functions of the minister

161

are based on his solidness of character, without which all that he says and does is but sounding brass and a clanging cymbal. He must look to it that his robe of office is unstained and his crown untarnished. This is, I think, the first function of the minister: to embody in his own life the high ideals for which religion and the profession of the ministry stand.

Second, it is the function of the modern minister to be diligent, alert and competent in administering the church over which he presides, as an institution subject to the ordinary laws that govern the success or the failure of any social organization. There is no divine law that operates automatically to overcome the difficulties of inadequacy in leadership and that guarantees the survival and success of the church — despite appearances to the contrary when some churches do, in fact, survive for a while the bungling of ministerial leadership. The exceptions have led to the erroneous conviction that any bright-eyed enthusiast can keep a church out of spiritual and material bankruptcy. But administration is both an art and a science, and the modern minister must be a master in this field. He cannot leave this function to the laity, who often confuse ecclesiastical management with the processes that prevail in the operation of a grocery store or a steel mill. Almost any layman suspects that he could manage the church better than the minister; and when the minister disdains organizational matters, he lends strength to this suspicion.

An administrator must have clarity of purpose. He must design organizational forms fitted to the purpose. He must co-ordinate activities. He must be able to delegate duties, and he must form the habit of following through to the conclusion of projects. The minister who sits back and waits for either Deacon Jones or God Himself to pilot the ship of church through troubled waters will find his ship floundering on the rocks, and himself appealing to the Grievance Committee of the Ministerial Union to right the imagined wrongs that the laity has allegedly heaped upon him.

The modern minister must be an administrator of high order, for he is dealing with a precious and delicate organization that responds quickly to intelligent leadership — and that reacts with equal rapidity to incompetence on the part of ministerial leadership.

In the third place, it is the function of the modern minister to serve the personal needs of his parishioners and others with the skill that comes from modern knowledge in many fields of learning, and with the broad and the sympathetic understanding that is born of wide experience with all sorts and conditions of people. Pious readings and the most eloquent prayers can no longer meet the needs of modern parishioners. Life today is highly complex, and personal problems are not easily dealt with. Wide and sympathetic understanding of all sorts of personal experiences is of the essence of the equipment of the modern minister. He must be basically and by nature tolerant, understanding and sympathetic.

Yet, while this basic equipment is essential, it is not enough. The modern minister must be thoroughly acquainted with the resources of his community, and be able to make intelligent referrals for those whom he counsels. He must know enough to distinguish between the fly-by-night movements and organizations, and those that are stable and reliable.

While the minister must not pose as a psychiatrist, he must know the art of counseling and be able to refer, when referral is indicated, to competent psychiatrists, as distinguished from advocates of shortcuts to knowledge, power and happiness. The needs in this field are far greater than most people realize. And these needs have not been met by informed ministerial leadership, with the result that innumerable cults (such as Christian Science and the various New Thought groups) have sprung up and flourished throughout the country. There is an abundance of valid knowledge in the field of counseling and of psychological problems in general, and the modern minister should be thoroughly acquainted with it. However, he must scrupulously avoid becoming a sectarian in the psychiatric field, where sectarianism flourishes even as it does in the field of religion.

The relationship of the minister to those who counsel with him must be on a highly professional level. He must maintain confidences, as do lawyers and doctors, even in the face of governmental pressure. And he must never become a source of community gossip. No relationship in life should be more sacredly guarded than that of the minister to his parishioners.

In serving the personal needs of his people, the work of the minister is not confined to personal relationships. In the so-called service of worship, a sort of group counseling is involved. This is why I am concerned about the carrying over into modern times of ancient moods, embodied in traditional language that has no meaning for modern-minded people. It is possible and it is desirable to meet the emotional and aspirational needs of modern congregations by the use of hymns, readings and language that are meaningful to people in modern society. What meaning has the symbol of the shepherd and the sheep on a thousand hills to people whose only contact with that meek animal is chops from a deep freezer? What meaning do plowshares and pruning hooks have in an age of tractors and combines? The symbols that were appropriate in a primitive Palestinian community no longer fit the life of modern industrial society. Hence the modern minister must strive to develop symbols and services that will do for modern people what ancient symbols and services did for ancient peoples. This is a function that the modern minister should perform with care, with dignity and with vision.

In the fourth place, the modern minister must represent his church — and the high ideals for which he stands — in the larger life of his community. This he must do on the level of informed and inspired leadership, and not on the level of clerical assistance to professional reformers or partisan politicians, nor yet mainly as a manipulator of "buzz sessions." And he must never succumb to the cheap publicity that accompanies pontifical pronouncements on matters about which he knows absolutely nothing and the championing of half-baked ideas and movements.

The minister owes it to his community to be active in civic affairs, and he owes it to his church and to himself to be fully informed on the civic affairs in which he engages. A reputation for sober judgment is prerequisite to effective community service. It is easy for a minister who is not fully informed on civic matters to get himself out on a limb, saw off the limb and fall on his back — whereupon his community leadership is ended or greatly handicapped.

In the age in which we live, national and world affairs impinge on the smallest community. Consequently, the modern minister must have knowledge of the conflicting theories that are battling for the mind of modern man and the movements that are attempting to capture him — mind, body and soul. One of the most pitiful spectacles I can think of is a supposedly modern-minded democratic liberal championing causes that are antithetical to every principle that a modern-minded democratic liberal is supposed to stand for. That happens in some cases where the minister in question has not done any rethinking or changed his mind for twenty-five years. I can account for this only on the basis of inadequate knowledge or the absence of rigorous thinking.

The modern minister must not only think straight on national and world issues, but he must be able to distinguish between the ideal and the possible. Ideality must be wedded to practicality. Moon-eyed visionaries can render no useful service to the life of their country. Good solid opinions, backed by factual information and geared to the idea of the possible, can make great headway in any modern community. But fragmentary information, brittle thought and fragile convictions can do little or nothing for any community.

The modern minister must be a tower of strength for the great ideals and movements that are striving to shape the life of the modern world in behalf of human dignity and decency, freedom and abundance, peace and tranquility. He cannot isolate himself from the great causes of his day, or retire to his tower and meditate on the woes of mankind.

Fifth and last, it is the function of the modern minister to preach as an evangel from the world of the imponderables — the world of justice, of mercy and of love.

One of my happy memories is that of once reading in a history of a Baptist Association in the South a reference to my grandfather, who was a Baptist minister. It read: "He preached as a very evangel from the Spirit World." Now, my conception of the content of the Spirit World would differ radically from that of my grandfather; but the world of the imponderables is a very real world to which the modern minister must have a profound loyalty.

Preaching is the most important function of the minister, and he should magnify his calling. I have very great sympathy with the old Virginia divine who arose in his study one day, paced the floor back and forth in great distress and exclaimed: "I can't preach, I have never preached, and I have never heard anybody who could preach!" So great was his feeling of the importance of preaching!

Preaching is the proclamation of profound conviction. And there can be no effective preaching without profound conviction. The science of homiletics can be learned; the art of public speaking can be acquired. But preaching is more than the science of homiletics and more than the art of public speaking. It grows out of the deepest experiences and the most solemn convictions of the preacher. It requires a genuine concern for the well-being of those to whom the preacher preaches, a deep concern for the welfare of the world in which they live, and the power to envision a society in which justice and mercy and love may yet reign supreme.

When the minister stands in the pulpit he must know no master other than his own profound convictions. He has no right to mental reservations and no duty to theological and ecclesiastical conventions. He stands in a direct relation to the world of the imponderables, and he must declare in no uncertain terms their claim on the life of everyone within the sound of his voice. It is not enough for the preacher to tell his hearers that they must repent as it were and believe in a measure or they will be damned to an extent. He must call them to complete repentance, to complete devotion, or warn them that they will be completely damned. In the pulpit there can be no compromise on justice and mercy and love.

There was never greater need than now for preaching that stirs the deeper emotions, fires the imagination and directs action into channels of righteousness. There is need for the preacher to call leaders of public opinion and officers of government to account for their actions at the bar of the highest values. There should be no place in the pulpit of today for time-servers or for preachers who lower their standards to conform to the convenience of leaders in labor or industry or politics. No man should be thought too high or too low to be called to account for his actions. Effective preaching not only proclaims justice and mercy and love; it also condemns in scathing terms injustice and brutality and hate.

All the virtues of Hebrew prophecy and Roman eloquence should come to fruition in the pulpit of the preacher today. No lesser goal should be that of the modern preacher, and no lesser achievement should give him satisfaction.

Between Man and Man

by Jack Mendelsohn

It was my good fortune in Jerusalem to spend an hour with
one of the most vivid of Israel's personalities, Martin Buber.
Buber is a brisk seventy-nine years of age. He has long since
earned the right of freedom from casual interviews. Fortunately
for me, a persuasive young official of the Israeli Foreign Office
phoned for my appointment. Martin Buber is a world citizen,
but he is also an Israeli patriot. The Foreign Office laid a duty
on his shoulders. He accepted. I was the beneficiary.

A thirty-minute interview was set for 9:30 A.M. at Buber's
home. The same morning I had an 8:30 appointment at the
Prime Minister's office to discuss Arab affairs within Israel with
the man who advises Ben-Gurion on such matters. The status
of Israel's Arab citizens is a point of fascination for me. The
Prime Minister's adviser is a fascinating man. I overstayed. It
was 9:20 when I ran down the steps of Israel's "White House"
and headed on foot, briskly, for Jerusalem's Talbiyeh section.

Jerusalem looms large in the consciousness of mankind, but
both old Jerusalem in Jordan and new Jerusalem in Israel are
surprisingly small towns. It is easy to find a designated "section"
of the new city. I was in Talbiyeh by 9:28. Finding a particular
street is a different matter. The streets wander in and out of one
another with an aimlessness that puts Boston to shame. There
are unique difficulties in getting information from other pedes-
trians. Frequently it is a language barrier. More often it is a
simple matter of ignorance. Most Jerusalemites can find their
own homes, even in the dark, but with so many important things
on their minds who can expect them to learn the street designa-
tions in an area where no pavement runs more than one hundred
yards without changing direction and name?

Reprinted by permission from Congress Weekly, *November 18,
1957, pp. 7-9.*

Experience sustained me. As soon as I knew that Buber's home could not be far from where I stood, I accosted the first passer-by and asked not for a street but for "the house of Martin Buber." The result was magnificent. I was pointed up one diagonal and down another. At 9:34 I paused before a rusty iron gate. Behind a tangle of bushes, shrubs and gnarled trees I could see the stucco of a venerable one-story house. From the gate to the porch was a matter of twenty strides, but the path was not designed for tall men. I walked it bent over, warily avoiding branches and hanging brambles. From within the house came the sound of a resonant voice speaking on the phone in Hebrew, punctuating the conversation with my name.

I was late. My whereabouts was in question. What a way to begin a dialogue with the world's greatest dialogical philosopher! But brazenness comes to those who travel. With my face set in its blandest expression I rang the bell. The door was opened by a husky woman who seemed to be in the midst of washing walls. She rolled her eyes at the mention of my name and ushered me immediately toward an adjoining room. I was met at the threshold by a bearded prophet.

Martin Buber is a gnomelike man, barely five feet tall, with a huge head and a magnificent, flowing, white beard. He looks like an ancient prophet, except for his eyes. I picture the eyes of ancient prophets as blazing with zeal. Buber's eyes are large, brown, soft and compassionate.

While I fumbled through an apology for being late, he led me toward the window of his study where we sat face to face across a small, round walnut table.

Buber's study deserves the skill of a Dickens for proper description: Victorian desk and divan, a lamp that must have been designed very shortly after Edison's invention of the electric bulb, random heaps of books, brochures, pamphlets and manuscripts. So this, I thought, is where the famous essays, lectures and volumes get written. No living man can claim a larger influence on the thought-life of his world than Martin Buber, yet this influence stems from the simple, cluttered surroundings of a

dusty study on a drowsy street in divided Jerusalem. No secre-
taries, no buzzer system, not even a typewriter.

Before I left, Buber talked of his personal situation. "Un-
happily," he said, "I seem to have become famous, especially in
America. Each day the mailman brings me bundles of mail which
I must answer myself. It is very discouraging." His face brightened with an after-thought. "I shouldn't complain. I never
dreamed that I would reach this age and still be capable of so
much work."

I had arrived late, and though my host showed no sign of
annoyance I wanted to launch the interview on a stimulating
note. Buber, I knew, had recently made a triumphal lecture tour
in the United States. *Time* and *Newsweek* had given him prominent coverage. It would be interesting to know: what did Dr.
Buber think of the religious revival in America? He moved to
the front of his chair, and his eyes brightened. He ran his fingers
through his beard and asked me if I wanted a personal answer.
When I nodded yes, he put another question: "What do you
mean by religious revival?"

"The religious revival we usually talk about in America," I
answered, "includes a great upsurge of church attendance and
much public piety."

"Ah," he said, "then I can tell you what I think. If a person
goes to church because it is a natural expression of that person's
desire to change his life in *all* respects — personal, social, economic, political — then his church attendance can be a manifestation of a genuine religious revival. But if it is just another
means of avoiding any real change, it is not religious revival but
the very opposite. I fear that much of the increased churchgoing
in America is of the latter type."

Was he asked this question many times in America?

Buber smiled. "No one in America asked me this question.
I met with all kinds of religious leaders, yet no one asked. It re-
minds me of one of Grimm's fairy tales I used to read as a boy.
A man was walking across a field. Suddenly the field opened,
and a pillar of flame arose. Within the fire there was a voice.
The man stood dumb before it. Soon the fire died down, and

the earth began to close. But just before it did, the voice said: 'If you had asked me something, I would have told you something.' If they had asked me something in America, I would have told them something."

By this time Buber was warming to the subject. "The old distinctions between religion and nonreligion are dead. Religion has nothing to do with church attendance as such, nor with doctrinal beliefs as such. These old distinctions are utterly meaningless in the present situation. Those who call themselves religious and those who call themselves nonreligious must join hands to find the first steps out of our human situation. In his readiness to do this, the agnostic or even the atheist may be more religious than his believing neighbor."

I suddenly realized that Buber was exercising such a hypnotic influence over me that I had completely neglected my notebook. Opening it, I shifted ground. Buber had called upon his fellow Jews to rise above their terrible memories of Nazi butchery. To underline his theory of reconciliation, he, who is alive only because he fled the Nazi horror in 1938, has repeatedly returned to Germany since the war's end to lecture in German universities. "What about Germany?" I asked, my ball-point pen poised.

"All my life I have been interested mostly in what is happening to young people. This is what interests me in Germany. In Germany, as everywhere else, we can divide the young people into three groups. First there are the indifferent ones: a very large group, as with all mankind. Then there are those who think their fathers did well in the Nazi era. They have a good conscience about Hitler and his works. This, I think, is a relatively small group. Then there are those who not only want to change but believe that change is possible. These are the hope of the future."

I had been scribbling furiously. Suddenly there was silence. When I looked up into Buber's face, he was smiling. "Mr. Mendelsohn," he said, "either you can take notes without really listening, or you can really listen without taking notes."

It was said without harshness. I firmly closed the notebook and placed it on the table. Buber, after all, is the creator of what he calls the "I-Thou relationship." Most men, he says, live in an

"I-It relationship" with life and with others, which bring separation, barrenness, hostility, fear. Only as a man begins to see
another as "Thou" rather than "It" — only then is true relationship and trust created. My notebook was an "It" standing between Buber and me. With the notebook down, it could be "I
and Thou" in both directions.

He picked up the thread of his thought. "Throughout the
world there is a front on which is being waged a secret, silent
battle between the desire to be on life's side and the desire to
destroy. This is the most important front of all — more important than any military, political or economic front. It is the
front on which souls are molded. Let me give you an example.
Three years ago I was invited to lecture at Göttingen University
in Germany. The old nationalistic student organizations had
been revived, and some weeks before my arrival they had demon-
strated noisily. It had nothing to do with my visit. It was just
the same old pre-Hitler fanaticism reasserting itself. After my
lecture, the officials led me from the university to the city square.
The place was packed with thousands of students who had gathered to give me an ovation. It was not because of anything I had
said in my lecture, but simply because to those students I was a
symbol of the humanizing trend they desperately want for their
own lives. This secret, silent battle is going on in the hearts of
the young everywhere. Our future hangs on its outcome."

My next question was obvious. "What can an individual do
to tip the balance?"

"No one can chart a day-by-day course of action for anyone
else. Life can only be determined by each situation as it arises.
Every person has his chance. From the time he gets up in the
morning until the time he retires at night, he has meetings with
others. Sometimes he even meets himself! He sees his family at
breakfast. He goes to work with others. He meets people in the
street. He attends gatherings with others. Always there are
others. What he does with each of these meetings is what counts.
The future is determined far more by this than by ideologies and
proclamations."

Buber confronts us with extreme simplicity. The human

situation, so-called, is reduced to a series of personal moral questions: How do I conduct myself in this moment with this person? What is my duty? What do I do next? Here, says Buber, is where the future is determined.

I told my host that I was deeply impressed by what he said, yet I found myself wondering what place he would give to political solutions. He swung around in his chair and gazed out the window. When he spoke, it seemed to be more to himself than to me. "I do not trust politicians, and not because they are evil men. But they are forced to view things in terms of their party and their nation. That is not enough."

He turned again to face me. "People have the real power. If people truly desired no atom war there would be no atom war, because the people would go to their politicians and say, 'We want no atom war!' And no politicians on earth, not even those in Russia, could refuse them."

The allotted time of my interview had long since run out. Buber showed no restlessness. I ventured another question. "What about Israeli youth? Where do they stand on this spiritual front?"

"The problem," he answered, "is a special one. The young people of Israel live in a situation that demands their first attention. For them it is a matter of sheer survival. The situation makes them politically absorbed. The situation must come first. The soul waits."

The significance of these words was renewed a few days later in a sober conversation with a young sabra (native-born Israeli). I asked him if many of the younger Israelis were doing original thinking in religion. "No one in Israel has time," he said. I reminded him of Buber. "He is a great man," was the answer, "but we have no time to listen. We are too busy."

Building a new country, surrounded by implacable enemies, explains the absorptions of young Israelis. I found myself wondering what absorbs our young people. I am not sure I know. Surely here, as in Israel, the soul waits. But for what?

I left the house of Martin Buber in a kind of daze. I knew

what is meant by his gift for embracing the "Thouness" of others. As we sat and talked, he seemed to take into account the silence behind my words as well as the words themselves. He had welcomed me into his soul and his thought. Somehow his very presence helped me to remember, as rarely before, that I too have a soul and a life of thought.

The grandeur of Martin Buber is not in his staggering output of literature, nor in his fame, nor in his theological influence. His grandeur is in the simple manner in which he tells us to take hold of life where we find it, to uncover hope in the way we think, feel, talk and act toward those we meet each day. This, he says, is how we give leadership to our leaders. This is how we restore health to a sick world.

Religion in the Schools

by Philip Schug

On April 20, 1958, the San Antonio *Express and News* had a Sunday feature article on religion in the public schools. The article was based on the opinions of six high school seniors who had been chosen to compose a Teen Sounding Board. None of the students knew what was to be discussed until they had assembled. We may assume that their expressed opinions represented their convictions.

The results were most interesting. Four of the six students favored compulsory courses in religion in the schools. Two favored elective courses. None objected. To judge from the article, all thought of the courses as teaching the Christian religion. "A person doesn't have to belong to any particular faith," said one student, "but he should be a Christian." (This quotation was used to close the article.) All the students seemed to believe that courses in religion should be given in the schools in order to reach children who had so far escaped church influence.

These students were probably typical. They will soon be determining policy in our community, and in a few years they will have children of their own in the school systems. Obviously they are unacquainted with the history of western man leading to the enunciation of the principle of separation of church and state. Apparently they have never thought through the consequences of formally turning our public schools into Protestant parochial schools. We must draw the conclusion that they have no deep sense of respect for extremely important rights of the individual.

These are weighty charges, and I would not lightly dismiss them with the assumption that these young people will see things differently when they mature. There is no evidence that their parents' attitudes differ significantly from theirs. Their parents are responsible for the operation of the public schools, and their passion for putting religion into the schools is restrained only by law. Moreover, in four years, some of the recent crop of seniors will return to teaching positions in the local school systems. They will be teaching the children of the seniors of five years ago. Where in this process do you find people with a different understanding and position?

Now it is true that there are no compulsory classes in sectarian religion in the public school curricula in San Antonio; but there are worship services, hymn singing, Bible reading, memory verses, prayers and short sermons in the classrooms. Many of the teachers are quite evangelistic, and some of the principals encourage their teachers to give the children more religion. Teachers, principals, parents and children seem to be agreed that the time to get at the children is when they are required by law and custom to be in the school classroom.

Let us suppose, now, that you are paying public school taxes and also, because of religious convictions, are supporting your children in a private school operated by your church. You willingly bear the double cost. Would you not be inclined to feel that there is something unfair about the fact that the Baptists and the Methodists have been allowed to take over the public schools as places in which they teach their religion? Would you not be inclined to insist that the public treasury also bear the cost of your private schools? It is bearing the costs of the Baptists' and the Methodists' schools; why should yours be discriminated against?

Again, let us suppose that you are Jewish, or Seventh Day Adventist, or Unitarian. You send your children to the public schools, but the religion that is taught them by their teachers is not your religion. Are you not inclined to resent the fact that your children are required by law to be in school, and are then subjected to religious training of which you do not wholly approve? If there were equally good private schools in which your religion were taught, or in which no religion was taught, would you not be inclined to send them there, providing the cost was no greater than your current school tax bill? Even if it were somewhat greater, would you not be tempted? But if the costs were wholly in addition to your present school taxes, would you not be inclined to anger, feeling that the majority groups were taking advantage of their numbers to charge you for spreading their religion, while at the same time practically capturing your children in their own private schools? If you were able, would you not pass laws eliminating religion from the public schools? Or, if that were not possible, would you not insist that the public treasury support schools in which your religion is taught, or in which no religion is taught?

Human justice, the ability to put yourself in the position of your neighbor, a sensitivity to the rights of others and a desire to keep group friction to a minimum — all suggest that schools maintained by the public, at public expense, for the children of all who wish to send them must be free of such divisive elements as religion and politics. Why, then, is there such overwhelming pressure in San Antonio — and, indeed, in many other parts of the country — to intensify and extend a program of religious education in the public schools?

The answer, I believe, has these major facets: (1) a failure to understand the place of the public school in the cultural life of the United States, (2) an ultimate rejection by many people of the principle of cultural pluralism, and (3) an ultimate rejection of — or failure to understand — the principles of democracy. Let us consider this third problem first.

Regardless of the form it takes, a democratic organization of people requires that the public institutions be operated without discrimination and without prejudice for the benefit of all. Because a democratic organization depends for its practical operation upon the agreement of majorities, those majorities must be restrained by law and custom from infringing upon rights guaranteed to all. Even a minority of one can, in theory, prevail against the oppressive, thoughtless and illegal action of a majority.

In this country we have reached agreement on several basic rights of citizens. Among these is the right to follow the religion of one's choice or to be free from the dictates and pressures of all organized religions. It follows, then, that the state may not establish one religion or any religion, may not use its coercive powers to command the attendance of any citizen at a religious ceremony, and may not allow religious organizations to make use of the legal machinery to infringe the rights of any citizen. A genuine concern for the rights of minorities in a plural culture — a culture in which there are many religious groups — requires that the state take a neutral position. These principles are well established in law, having been tested many times in the courts.

In public schools, the duly constituted authorities are charged with responsibility to see that no religious exercises take place in the schools that would infringe the rights of citizens. School boards, superintendents, principals and teachers are responsible for maintaining religiously neutral schools. Their first civic duty, as employees of the state, is to maintain the principles upon which the state is founded and sustained. They should be zealous to make democracy work, and they should resign their jobs rather than allow the pressures of any group, even a very large majority, to prevail over the rights of a minority, however small. They should be so imbued with the philosophy of democracy that they could not allow even their own religious convictions to be imposed upon the captive audience that the police powers of the state provides in the public school classroom.

Now, you may well ask me, where one can find such a teacher, administrator or school board member? Frankly, I do not know; but the principles of democracy, as they apply to this situation, are so clear that they cannot possibly be misunderstood when they are searched out and set forth by people of ordinary intelligence. Yet the great majority of educators either do not understand them or reject them. Which is it? Or is it both?

I think it is both, and I suspect that the rejection of democratic principles lies at the heart of the failure to search out and make clear the principles upon which a public school system must be based if it is to long endure. When high school seniors, for example, can justify their demands for compulsory religion in public schools by saying (as reported in the *Express and News* article), "A lot of kids don't come from Christian homes," it is almost conclusive proof that their teachers have taught them bigotry and hatred of those who differ from them, instead of the self-discipline required of all in a democratic framework. A teacher, after all, teaches what he or she is. If the teachers of these students were themselves imbued with democratic principles, it is difficult to see how they could have failed so completely to put those principles across. Only two of the six students showed any real concern for the rights of others, and one of those was won over by the rest. "If you would make it compulsory," she said finally, "then make it compulsory in junior high school, where the kids are more impressionable."

This rejection of the principles of democracy goes hand in hand with the rejection of the principle of cultural pluralism. For many years we were an immigrant country, welcoming people from all places in the world. We were a haven for the homeless, but we were far from a heaven for the weary. These national and religious groups formed an explosive mixture. Hatred, bigotry, discrimination and all forms of legal oppression were known among us — and, indeed, are still known. Yet regardless of cruelties on the local level, where bigot clashed with bigot, the state and the nation had to adopt a policy of live-and-let-live among the cultural groups. The larger the governmental unit, the more firmly accepted was the principle of cultural pluralism.

In the field of education, this principle was gradually clarified and applied. Its latest extension is in the integration of the races, and the fiercest resistance is met, as usual, at the local level. There, it seems, the various cultural groups would almost rather kill each other than see each other granted equal rights.

Some of the earliest battles over religion in the schools centered on whether cultural and religious groups had the right to establish their own private schools, in which they might teach their own philosophies or religious tenets. Thanks must go to the Roman Catholics for early and persistent demands that the state have no monopoly in the field of education and that the public schools remain religiously neutral. Cultural pluralism was thus assured. Hundreds of suits have been entered against school boards which have permitted and encouraged sectarian religious activities in public school classrooms. One hundred years of legal suits have established, for practical purposes, that even the reading of the Bible without comment is sectarian teaching, since Protestants have one Bible, Catholics another and Jews still another. (In the last twenty years, of course, the Roman Catholics have completely changed their tactics and now give every encouragement to Protestants who want to load their public schools with Protestant parochialism.)

Religious neutrality is essential in the public schools if they are to sponsor the principles of cultural pluralism. But the history of the public schools is that most administrators and teachers inevitably inject sectarian religion into the classrooms. The ideal of cultural pluralism seems, on the whole, to be abhorrent to educators. Perhaps they want to educate the whole man, as they often claim; but they often appear to be inclined toward "soul-saving" — and one cannot be both a soul-saver and a champion of cultural pluralism.

As I see it, then, public school administrators and public school teachers have little regard for democratic principles and little real regard for cultural pluralism. In San Antonio, at least, they seem to reject these principles, for their graduates believe that the Christian religion should be compulsory for all public school children, and seem never to have heard of the basic rights of the individual nor of the principle of separation of church and state. Some educators, I suppose, were appalled when they read the opinions of the Teen Sounding Board, but they can hardly deny that the students are the product of their teaching.

The final reason for the overwhelming pressure, in San Antonio and elsewhere, to intensify and extend programs of religious education in the public schools lies in a failure to understand and to accept the place of the public school in the cultural life of the United States.

The public school is aimed at giving a common education to the children of parents from all walks of life and from every variety of cultural background. This means that the parents must accept the principles of the public school and must trust it to enlighten their children and train them in a basic respect for their neighbors. This trust can be fulfilled, and this purpose can be achieved, only with the voluntary acceptance of limitations by the teachers, school administrators and the public in general. The public schools must not, for example, favor one religion over another nor function in such a way as to establish one or any religion. The moment they do so, they violate the public trust, and perseverance in such actions will ultimately destroy them. This destruction is inevitable, because no public school in our pluralistic culture can undertake religious education without opening up the question of whose philosophy and whose religion will be taught. Agreement is impossible, and failure to achieve agreement will split the schools into competing systems.

We are closer than most of us think to this destruction of the public schools. I mentioned earlier that the Roman church had changed its tactics and now encourages Protestant parochialism in the public schools, after one hundred years of hard-fought court cases in opposition to it. This change of tactics was formally announced by the Roman hierachy in November 1948, when it stated that "Separation of Church and State has become the shibboleth of doctrinaire secularism" and pledged the church to "work peacefully, patiently and perseveringly" for its destruction. Turning the public schools into Protestant parochial schools is the first step in the attempted destruction. Protestants have been overwhelmed with gratitude for the encouragement, grants of money, partnerships in lawsuits and collaborative clerical pressure they have received.

The second step was inevitable; and its form appeared clearly on April 8, 1958, when the National Catholic Education Association, with ten thousand delegates convened in Philadelphia, openly demanded public support for its parochial schools equal to that for public schools. If I were a Catholic, I would demand such support too. After all, the schools are all parochial schools anyway! Why should one be favored over another? Multiply this by the number of zealous sects, and you see the end to which public school shortsightedness is tending.

The only alternative seems clear. The champions of the public schools, together with the public school administrators and teachers, must accept a realistic place in the total structure of the culture. They must voluntarily limit the scope of the public school teaching to that which does not generate its own destruction. They must accept, rather than reject, the concept of cultural pluralism. They must accept, rather than reject, democratic principles of operation.

Let me close with a famous quotation from the writings of L. P. Jacks, an English philosopher, on the subject of religion in the schools:

Not long ago I met one of our great schoolmasters — a veteran in that high service. "Where in your time-table do you teach religion?" I asked him. "We teach it all day long," he answered. "We teach it in arithmetic, by accuracy. We teach it in language, by learning to say what we mean — 'yea, yea and nay, nay.' We teach it in history, by humanity. We teach it in geography, by breadth of mind. We teach it in handicraft, by thoroughness. We teach it in astronomy, by reverence. We teach it in the playground, by fair play. We teach it by kindness to animals, by courtesy to servants, by good manners to one another, and by truthfulness in all things. We teach it by showing the children that we, their elders, are their friends and not their enemies." "But what," I said, "about the different denominations? Have you no trouble with the parents?" "None at all," he replied; "we have half a dozen denominations. But we treat the children, not as members of this church or that, but as members of the school, and we show them that, as members of the school, in work and in play, they are members of one another."[1]

(1) Lawrence Pearsall Jacks, *A Living Universe*, London, Hodder and Stoughton, Ltd., 1924, pp. 50-51. Cited in *Great Companions*, Robert French Leavens, ed., Boston, Beacon Press, 1941, Vol. II, pp. 616-17.

The Changing South: Revolution or Reconciliation?

by Edward A. Cahill

Change is a universal characteristic of life. One might say that change is a fundamental law of life, that not to change is to die. In one sense, the fact that the South is changing should not excite any special comment. Yet even the casual observer is struck by the depth and impact of social change in the South. For some reason, the changes which are occurring throughout the region, although not unique in themselves, seem significantly serious in a unique way. The changes which characterize the changing South might be described as regional reflections of national change, and yet somehow they are different.

The most dramatic and traumatic change in the South has been the tremendous shift from a completely agrarian society with a semifeudalistic character to one which is attempting to strike a balance between industry and agriculture, between an urban culture and an agrarian society. This has meant more than mere industrialization. It has meant a sudden shifting of values — the destruction of old values and the building of a new value system before the old has departed. This has been happening all over America, but in the South it is happening at a highly accelerated rate and right now.

The rapid advance in electrification, for instance, has had widespread implications. It has meant that even the areas which are predominantly rural have been saturated with urban values imported by radio, television and drive-in movies. All these changes — electrification, agriculture to industry, rural to urban

A slightly different version of this article was published in Phylon, *The Atlanta University Review of Race and Culture, July 1958, pp. 199-207.*

— have produced concomitant changes in individual and family life. The changes in the family highlight and symbolize the problem. Increased mobility available cheaply to all, the resultant lack of geographical stability, the tension between old and new values — these have fragmented family life. The old homogeneity is gone, and nothing has taken its place.

Similar changes are taking place all over the world. With fairness it can be pointed out, as it often is, that every problem facing the South is a national if not a world problem. Ralph McGill, editor of the Atlanta *Constitution*, has pointed out that what we are going through in the South is a worldwide revolution which has come to focus in our own backyard on the problem of race. He goes on to say:

> Many a sincere, average deep-South Southerner does not know, or refuses to admit, that world forces are at work in the American race problem as they are in Asia and Africa. Somehow, to him, his present harassments are all a sinister business brought on by an organization called the NAACP. He feels that a proper government would put it in jail or order it to go away, and then everything would again be as it was.[1]

One of the paradoxes of this situation is that those who shout the loudest and who put up the money for the White Patriots and the Citizens' Councils unwittingly have been those most responsible for bringing the problems of the South into sharp and critical focus. They are the ones who have organized industrial development committees, who have initiated programs of special privilege for new industry, who have gone north seeking venture capital. As a result of their energy and initiative, the South has been electrified, urbanized and industrialized at an unprecedented rate. This fact above all others has brought the problem of race into sharp and critical focus.

As I see it, there are two reasons, among others, which make the problem of change different in the South from what it is or has been in other parts of the country. (It is always dangerous

---

(1) Ralph McGill, "The Angry South," *The Atlantic Monthly*, April 1956, p. 34.

to pick out one or two special reasons to explain a phenomenon of social change, and only an amateur would venture to do so. Yet, as I have lived in the South and tried to understand what was happening around me, these two factors appeared to be profoundly significant. Perhaps they were highlighted in my mind because they are so often overlooked.)

The first reason involves the unique history of this region. The South has developed a culture of its own, with its own supporting mythology and its own identity, which takes emotional precedence to national identity. The second reason involves change. Change has been long delayed and is most recent in the Southland. The rate of change has been more rapid than in other parts of the country. The accelerated rate of change characteristic of this region puts the problem here on a different level. It is not only a quantitative matter of degree of difference — the change has been so rapid, so universal and so recent that the difference is, in effect, one of kind.

Now, as to the first reason, that of the separate regional culture: during "The War," the South, which was basically a frontier territory just snatched from the forests and from the Indians, gained an identity of its own. The War rapidly produced and crystallized a local regional patriotism and a highly developed sense of national consciousness. All nations have a supporting mythology; and the South, in the stress of The War, assembled a body of myth as its supporting mythology. In defeat and reconstruction, this mythology was about all that was left, and although it has been discredited in large measure by southern historians and scholars, shreds of it still remain to confuse the South as it faces up to its contemporary crisis.

The South is the only region in the United States where it is important to apologize for not having been born in it. Whenever I have had occasion to speak on a subject that might conceivably touch the sensitivities of the South, I have felt it important to introduce my remarks by stating, "I'm not a native-born Southerner. I'm from the North, and we had better understand that I understand that." Then I have been free to go on as an alien and an outsider, and personal courtesy and a great deal of generosity in the reception of my opinions has been extended me. The fact that the South is a separate culture in America with its exclusive mythology, that it is a nation within a nation, is one of the significant factors in understanding the dimension and depth of the current problem of race.

As to the second reason, the rapid and recent change, not much needs to be added. Change is all around us. Boom talk is in the air; it is the thing of which we as a region are most proud, and at the same time most anxious. The chamber of commerce atmosphere, the industrial development committees, the weekly reports on growth, the constant talk of perimeter problems and metropolitan development — all indicate how recent the change is, and how suddenly it has come upon us, and how deep and hidden are the effects.

We are all concerned with race, that volatile problem which is the focal point of all that we have been saying. Everywhere we turn in our attempts to meet the challenge of change, we face the problem of race. It is not too much to say that race is the focal point of a social, cultural, worldwide revolution. We are all concerned that this explosive problem be met creatively and constructively, not only in the South, but in the country as a whole. It can be said with some assurance that history will not be turned back on this point. Many of those who shout loudly today in defense of the status quo will admit in private that they recognize the inevitability of change — and of the specific patterns of change which are in process in the area of race relations in the South today. The South will either meet this problem with integrity and principle, or it will sabotage its own destiny as a great region taking its rightful place in the United States of America.

There has been a lot of talk about moderation and gradualism. The word "moderation" is a good word. It has an appealing sound to those who are committed to the democratic process, to those who deplore violence. It smacks of evolution and gradualism — the easy, comfortable slipping from one position to another with a minimum of dislocation of familiar landmarks. Moderation suggests a balanced approach, the use of intelligence and reason in solving human problems. For all these reasons it is too bad that the word has become perverted as it is applied to the problem of desegregation in the South today. Those who use it fail to understand that desegregation in the deep South is not a problem of implementation to be worked out by partners, white and Negro. This makes much of what they have to say irrelevant, if not misleading.

The Citizens' Councils, the Ku Klux Klan, the states' rights groups and the die-hard state officials of the hard-core states all shout open hysterical defiance of the Constitution and the Supreme Court. By their violence and their threats of violence, by their persistent and powerful attack upon all who stand for compliance, they have created a situation marked by the open confrontation of seemingly irreconcilable opposites.

It is true that a region's way of life cannot be changed overnight. Everyone who approaches the problem in a reasonable frame of mind realizes that violence is to be deplored and that gradual change is the order of the day. But this does not mean that no action toward change should be made. A "plea both to Northerners and Southerners and especially to Negro leaders for moderation in their attitudes toward this difficult problem and in the interpretation of those words, 'deliberate speed,' "[2] makes no sense when the speed is zero.

We hear the voices of sweet reasonableness quoted everywhere around us. A prominent educator says, "I'm opposed to the extremists on both sides." William Faulkner calls for a "moratorium on social change in the area of race relations." All this is grist to the mill of the segregationist, who will tolerate only one kind of moderation — the kind that means no change at all.

The liberal who prides himself on considering both sides of a question and who tries to understand even those with whom he disagrees is particularly susceptible to the voices of sweet reasonableness, to the sin of moderation. Perhaps we should

---

(2) Agnes E. Meyer, "Race and the Schools," *The Atlantic Monthly,* January 1958, p. 30.

look deeper and ask a few questions. Who has been *im*moderate?
The assumption behind most of what I hear in this vein is that
both sides have been immoderate. Is the assumption correct?

Has the Supreme Court been immoderate? Governor Griffin
of Georgia says it has, and habitually labels its decisions as illegal. But the Supreme Court has simply required the acceptance
of the constitutional principle of equality and called for its application to the admission of pupils to the public schools. It also
requires "good faith" on the part of public officials who have
sworn to uphold the Constitution of the United States, of their
intention to comply with the accepted principles of equality. Is
this immoderate extremism? According to Governor Griffin and
Senator Eastland, it is.

What about the Dixiecrat Manifesto? Is this moderation?
Talking about moderation out of one side of the mouth and
calling for open defiance of the law out of the other side is not
moderation by any stretch of casuistry. Its real effect is to encourage the hoodlum element to the kind of violence that occurred in Tuscaloosa and Little Rock. How can you legally
disobey the law? Is open incitement to the disobedience of the
law by officials of government moderation? Law and order is a
delicate thing. When constituted authorities encourage defiance
of the law, the Court and the Constitution, we should not be
surprised when hoodlums take the law into their own hands.
We should not be surprised, but let us be sure to place the responsibility where it belongs — upon those who openly and
defiantly subvert the orderly process of law.

Has the National Association for the Advancement of Col-
ored People been immoderate? In my opinion, and I have
observed their program at close hand for more than six years,
they have exemplified the epitome of moderation and gradualism.
They have practiced the true democratic approach to the solution of a tense and difficult problem. If any group has ever been
goaded into violent extreme action, it is the NAACP. They have,
with unbelievable patience, resisted the temptation to strike
back. Step by step they have proceeded with litigation in the
courts to establish the rights of Negroes. That is, or should be,

the approved democratic method for minorities to follow in seeking redress for the wrongs they suffer. What other "moderate method" is open to them?

Talk of moderation in the context of the South today is irrelevant and diversionary when it means ceasing to press by legal means for the recognition that the Constitution of the United States applies across the land to all peoples. How slowly can we go without nullifying the Constitution? Those who talk about "taking it easy" ignore the many years since Emancipation. They ignore the long, costly, patient litigation — the moderate nonviolent approach of the Negro people in their century-long struggle to gain recognition as first-class citizens.

A special burden rests upon Southern leadership when they talk moderation. Before they can be taken seriously, they must give evidence that they accept the Constitution as it has been applied to the segregation problem — not that they like it, but that they accept it — and that in "good faith" they are proceeding, or even planning to proceed, with reasonable speed to implement the Court's decision. The minimum we have a right to expect from our elected and appointed officials is a practical program of compliance based on relative local factors, and a time table for carrying out the program. Without this bare minimum, talk of moderation is irrelevant and diversionary. And this is the real "sin of moderation": it is a mouthing of platitudes for the purpose of postponing the day of reckoning, of escaping the obligation to apply a basic principle of democratic justice.

Agnes E. Meyer has correctly pointed out that "the greatest danger to the public school system is the legislation passed in four states, Virginia, South Carolina, Mississippi, and Georgia, to close the schools rather than allow one Negro child to enter a white school."[3] This is the real threat to American education — the irresponsible threat by those who hold political power to wreck the public schools rather than comply with the Supreme Court of the United States. In my opinion, this is the kind of extremism and immoderation that should be attacked. Senator

---

(3) *Ibid.*, p. 33.

Lehmann of New York, in a speech replying to the Dixiecrat Manifesto, put it this way:

> The substance of the matter is that a vast number of people in the southern States were and are being denied the equal protection of the laws, and were being set apart, and treated as pariahs in our society in access to public facilities supported by general tax revenues. Who can possibly justify the continuance for one needless moment of this intolerable discrimination, of this oppression?

None of us wants violence; and it is too bad that these very fine words — "gradualism" and "moderation" — have been appropriated and misused by those who would prevent all action. It is a fact that these words are now used to sabotage programs of action. In the context of the South today, talk of gradualism or moderation means do nothing, sit on your hands and wait.

To describe the other alternatives open to us, let me use the terms "revolution" and "reconciliation." Both deal with change. Revolution, as I shall use it, describes rapid change to the point of explosion. Reconciliation, as I shall use it, describes a nonexplosive manner of dealing with an explosive situation.

In the long past of man's history, change of any considerable dimension has almost always meant revolution. In one sense, the history of mankind might be likened to a series of volcanic explosions: tremendous thrusts of an explosive nature, then the gradual cooling of the hot lava until the pressure underneath is built up again to the point of a new explosion. Democracy represents a gigantic experiment in government designed to make change possible without explosion or revolution. Built into our system of democratic government are mechanisms of gradual change short of explosion.

It is something like atomic energy. In an atom bomb, fissionable material is brought together, unleashed and allowed to go uncontrolled. The uncontrolled nature of the reaction constitutes the explosion. When atomic energy is used for power, the same process takes place, but controls are injected so that the process is channeled into constructive directions. This is what I mean by reconciliation. Democracy *controls* change. It does so by making a virtue of nonconformity and heresy, and incorporating into its political mechanism a nonexplosive method of handling the explosive situations of social change.

Will there be revolution? That is to say, will there be violent explosion, bloodshed and civil strife, with all the attendant risk to the entire social fabric of the region? Or will there be reconciliation, controlled change — the harnessing of the dynamic of history in building a regional culture which is in gear with the evolutionary development of our national culture? This is the basic question facing the leadership of the South.

Concerned about the record of revolutionary noncompliance in the hard-core states, we are inclined to forget the strong, positive, deeply rooted factors in the culture and mythology of the South which will contribute to the reconcilation of the race problem. As Wilbur Cash points out in his amazingly penetrating and objective book, *The Mind of the South,* the Southerner possesses much that is positive that will be brought to bear upon the crisis. Here are a few of these deeply rooted positive factors which must be kept in mind when we "view with alarm."

In the South there is a deep conviction of human worth and dignity. Here we find the last stronghold of individualism. It was here in the South that the tree of liberty was nurtured. It was the South that produced Jefferson, Madison, Patrick Henry and Andrew Jackson. All this is part of the very soil of the region, and it is a part of the mythology of which the true Southerner is most proud.

Also, in the South there is a respect for law and order, as the sons of the South have proven in peace and in war. And there is the religion of the South. Parts of it do not appeal to the sophisticated; but looking at the region as a whole, we find a simple, uncomplicated, unreflective devotion to "religion."

These three factors work together. The mythology of the South tells the Southerner that man is a creature of dignity and worth, that he is capable of glory. The Constitution, which the Southerner helped write and to which he is loyal, tells him that the Negro is a man. His simple unreflective religion tells him that all men are the children of God and are brothers.

Man is capable of glory. All men are equal. The Negro is a man.

At the moment, this compound has thrown the Southerner into confusion. His spurious rationalizations based on his false mythology are falling apart. The foundations have been shattered. His own need for inner consistency and unity is the forgotten ally of change through reconciliation. It is the forgotten element when we "view with alarm." We forget that the people of Clinton, Tennessee — people who favored segregation — voted four to one for law and order on the day following the beating of the Baptist minister. When we view with alarm, we should remember the forgotten allies deep in the heart of the South: the tradition of liberty and freedom, the dignity of man, the loyalty to law, and the simple, all-pervading religion of the South.

Revolution or reconciliation? Too much has been set in motion in the South to stop now.

We can be reasonably sure that the changing South will continue to change, and that it will change for the better, and that as it faces up to its future, its virtues will overcome its faults. The demagogues and the courthouse boys are fighting a desperate rear-guard action, and they know it. Few great problems are solved outright. People of goodwill will go on ameliorating them, reconciling them, until finally they cease to be major problems. This process of amelioration, of reconciliation through the democratic method of controlled change, is under way. The handwriting is on the wall. The day is not far off when all men in this great nation will face each other as brothers with dignity, with glory and with justice.

Religion and Ethics in Business Decisions

by William R. Odell

The subject of religion and ethics in business decisions is intricate, and one might view it from several perspectives. I am deliberately choosing a viewpoint for this article that will emphasize the problems and difficulties in the situation, rather than the progress that has unquestionably been achieved. I am not a pessimist, but I believe that a word of caution is needed for those who feel that, if businessmen would only take their religion and their ethics to the office with them on weekdays, all would be well. It is, of course, supremely important that businessmen do this. But the problem is much less simple than this formula implies.

Relatively few businessmen are deliberately unethical (and this malady is by no means peculiar to businessmen). A much larger number are carelessly or unwittingly unethical. The principal manifestation of this is in the sphere of business entertainment and business gifts. It is easy to exaggerate the importance of these practices, but perhaps they warrant a few brief observations.

The entertainment of customers and suppliers, and the sending of gifts, are old practices. They range all the way from frequent, extravagant entertainment to the sending of a box of nuts at Christmas. The purposes range all the way from improper influence to the simple desire to keep one's name in the recipient's mind. These practices were, I believe, enormously encouraged by the Excess Profits Tax. One result of this tax was that, in effect, the government often paid ninety per cent of the cost. Many expenses of marginal value thus appeared to be a bargain, and many businessmen felt they would be derelict in their duty if they failed to take advantage of the situation.

Business entertainment and gifts have become very much a matter of course with many persons. I believe that a large proportion of these activities are innocent in intent and free of improper effect. Nevertheless, they are wrong in principle, and both givers and recipients should cooperate in abolishing them.

The businessmen with whom we are concerned, however, have neither chosen nor drifted into unethical behavior. On the contrary, they have an intense desire to be moral and ethical. The problem that confronts them — and it is a crucial ethical dilemma — is that of identifying the moral and ethical course from among the tangle of alternatives. This is, I believe, the most difficult and baffling aspect of the entire subject.

It is, I think, generally conceded that the business executive of today, as he grows increasingly professional in attitudes and status, sees more relevance of ethical considerations to his daily work than did the business leaders of an earlier and more rugged period. The great majority of businessmen today actually do what they conceive to be the ethical thing. But how does one identify the ethical course in any given situation?

It is my conviction that the ethical course can be determined by each individual only in terms of his own individual personal responsibility as he sees it. There is no formula for determining which business viewpoints are moral and which are not. I believe that personal responsibility is virtually synonymous with personal morality, and that the acid test of the moral and the ethical course is whether the individual conscience is satisfied.

In stressing the unique role of individual personal responsibility, I do not wish to deny the benefits of group thinking on these issues. Doubtless a group can often decide, by discussion and by democratic procedures, what is the moral and ethical course. This process may also serve to educate the less morally aware members of the group. On the other hand, the morality of a group may be lower than that of its more ethically conscious members. In any event, individual personal responsibility is the indispensable foundation, even of group decisions. There is no substitute for it.

For a number of reasons, the concept of personal responsibility has weakened in recent years. The growth of the size of institutions of all kinds, from the government down, has withdrawn the individual further and further from direct personal confrontation with the issues. And the further the individual is removed from such confrontation, the less clear become the morality and the ethics of any given decision. Personal responsibility is also weakening from disuse. More and more, people seem to go to church, *not* for help in meeting their responsibilities, but for relief from them. In other types of group thinking and group action there is the same danger: that the individual will tend to shift his own responsibility to the collective shoulders of the group. If a group has good and effective leadership, the result may be satisfying; without it, the group and its members may fail to meet their responsibilities. And leadership, in turn, is the exercise of personal responsibility by one or a few individuals.

The problem of identifying the moral or ethical course, in short, is the problem of recognizing one's personal responsibility. But to solve this, we must also distinguish the often obscure boundary line between issues of morals and issues of judgment.

Each of us, from time to time, has heard a sermon in which the minister has presented as a moral and religious issue a matter we regard as strictly a matter of judgment. But let us not be quick to criticize. As businessmen we must recognize that a minister is justifiably concerned about many business issues. At the same time, the minister should recognize that he may not always be qualified, by information or experience, to form a final judgment on these issues. He must be careful, therefore, not to move an issue mistakenly from the sphere of judgment to the sphere of morals. But the boundary is obscure — and this may well be an understatement.

Let me offer as an example the much-vexed issue of inflation. Some people take the position that, for one or another reason, continuing inflation is inevitable. But I believe that the last word on this was said by the *London Economist* in an editorial in September 1951: "The proposition that inflation is inevitable is not an acknowledgment of economic determinism but a political judgment that the will to control inflation has disappeared."

My personal view is that inflation is a moral issue. By undermining the value of savings, inflation deters individuals from the effort to provide for their personal obligations. Personal responsibility is thereby undermined, and individuals are demoralized. Even the degree of inflation suffered in this country has sufficed to create the philosophy of the "fast buck," which goads us to delinquency. We should not forget that it was primarily the disastrous German inflation of the 1920s that destroyed personal responsibility and thus set the stage for Hitler.

Yet there are many high-minded people, both businessmen and economists, who either are tolerant of inflation or actually favor it. Their viewpoint sometimes rests on the belief (which I do not share) that a relatively stable economy with full employment is attainable only with some degree of continuing inflation. To me, inflation is a moral issue; to these men it is a matter of judgment. We disagree profoundly, but I do not feel justified in condemning their opinions as immoral.

Let us follow this problem of inflation into a specific business decision. Many important labor contracts in recent years have included two provisions for "escalation" of wage rates: a provision by which wage rates automatically rise with increases in living costs, and an annual, automatic "improvement factor," which purports to give labor its share of increasing productivity. I believe it is generally conceded that, in recent years, the effect of these provisions has been to reinforce inflation. If a management believes, as I do, that inflation is a moral issue, what is its moral duty with respect to these labor contract provisions? Is its moral duty — aside from considerations of judgment — to resist their application, even to the extent of undergoing a strike? This is an uncomfortable question to answer.

Or take another example, one which is serious today and which bids fair to become much more serious in the near future. This is the issue of protective tariffs. Production costs, led by wages, have now reached such a level in the United States that exporting is extremely difficult and importing extremely attractive. The time is approaching when we shall have to decide whether or not to promote a substantial increase of tariff protection in order to maintain wage levels in this country. Will this be an issue of judgment or an issue of morality? I happen to favor the free-trade viewpoint, but the answer to this question is far from obvious to me.

But granted that this boundary line between judgment and morality is shadowy, there remain innumerable business decisions which clearly *do* involve ethical and moral considerations. Here we are confronted with the problem, not of whether to do the ethical and moral thing, but of how to determine the ethical and moral course. The Gospel warns us that "no man can serve two masters," but the businessman must attempt to serve not less than four: his shareholders, his customers, his employees and the community. As he makes his decisions, the business executive must strike a fair balance among these often conflicting interests. There is perhaps no simpler way of stating the businessman's problem.

It is easy to say that there should be no conflict among these interests, that what is best for one is best for all. Theoretically, this is true; but it is rarely a practical answer to a specific issue. If a lawyer should find himself representing conflicting interests, ethics would require him to withdraw from all but one. But the businessman has no escape. And there are relatively few decisions in which the moral case among the conflict of interests is so clear that sincerely moral men will fully agree on the proper course. The proper decision is frequently indeterminate — on strictly moral grounds. Judgment must play a part.

Let me offer two examples, one very simple, the other very complex:

1 —— Let us assume that a large amount of money is required by the principal hospital in a city in which the company has a large plant. The company has, I believe, a clear moral responsibility to contribute to this need in an appropriate amount. But what *is* the appropriate amount? This decision requires a careful weighing of conflicting interests, and there may

well be a wide range of opinion among men of unquestioned morality. The issue is no longer purely and clearly a moral one, and the result may not wholly satisfy the moral conscience of all who participate in the decision.

2 —— Our complex example is a continual one: how shall the responsible executive of a company allocate the benefits produced by the business? What part of earnings should be distributed as dividends to shareholders, and what part retained for improving and protecting the company? What benefits and concessions should be allotted to employees? What prices should be established to customers? What expenditure and effort should be devoted to community purposes, local or national?

The executive may, in fact, have very little freedom of choice in determining this distribution. Selling prices must be at levels at which an adequate volume of the product can be sold. The labor union which represents the employees may be strong enough virtually to impose its terms. The resulting earnings may or may not be adequate to maintain the financial stability of the company; the test of this is whether the company is able at all reasonable times to attract additional capital if required.

We have started with what appears to be the moral and ethical question of a fair distribution of the benefits produced, but we have ended with the question of adequate financial strength, which is clearly a question of judgment. I am not implying that judgment should ever prevail over morality: no clear moral principle should be violated by any business decision under any circumstances. If a business cannot survive without violating moral principles, it should not survive. But one does not necessarily violate morality by imposing sacrifices on one or all of the several interests, if judgment indicates that the sacrifice will be for the long-run benefit of these interests.

This scrambling together of elements of both morality and judgment in matters involving conflicting interests results, to a large degree, from the direction of our economic and political development. As our society becomes more highly organized and our institutions more numerous and more complex, conflicting interests become more numerous and more baffling in their implications. The issues become further and further removed from the direct concern of personal responsibility — and so from personal morality and conscience. The moral implications become clouded and become inextricably entwined with those of judgment. It is difficult to escape the feeling that there is in operation a sort of law of diminishing moral visibility: that as institutions — government, labor, business and all others — become larger, more numerous and more complex, the moral course becomes increasingly indeterminate and obscure.

What can guide the business executive in this maze of conflicting interests and complex interrelationships of morality and judgment? He cannot, in spite of the difficulties, escape his individual personal responsibility to apply his religion and his ethics to his daily problems. In fact, only as he appreciates and faces these practical difficulties can he apply them effectively. In the last analysis, his guide must be his individual, personal conscience; he must simply do the best he can to satisfy his own religious and ethical convictions.

The businessman is often criticized for what appears to be a disregard of ethics; but the decisions in question may actually be errors of judgment. The economic injustice and distress from which we suffer from time to time result, I believe, from errors of judgment by businessmen much more than from unethical conduct. One might say that critics of businessmen credit them with less regard for ethics and with better judgment than they generally possess.

I am keenly aware that I have raised many more questions than I have answered. But I do not wish to close on a note of pessimism. I do believe that there are at least two constructive influences at work. The businessmen of this generation are increasingly aware of the relevance of moral and ethical considerations to business decisions that have traditionally been regarded as solely matters of judgment. And more and better education of all the conflicting interests — stockholders, employees, customers and the general public — will greatly facilitate for businessmen the application of moral and ethical considerations.

The influence of these two factors have, in recent years, much improved the application of religion and ethics to business decisions, and they will surely continue to do so.

Birth Control: Dogma and Dilemma

by Alvah W. Sulloway

In matters of faith and morals, the Roman Catholic church claims infallibility for its Popes and sets all eternity as the duration of its decrees. Yet it has exhibited to the world, in its pronouncements on birth control, a remarkable series of intellectual gyrations. In 1930, for example, Pius XI's encyclical *Casti Connubii (Christian Marriage)* condemned birth control by the use of contraceptives as intrinsically immoral. Twenty-one years later, his successor, Pius XII, interpreted the earlier pronouncement in such a way as to permit family limitation by the "natural" or Rhythm method. The efforts of Catholic writers to explain and defend this metaphysical legerdemain have not clarified the picture; they have only added inconsistency to confusion.

Theologically, the Catholic doctrine on birth control stems from the church's concept of natural law. The primary end of intercourse, says the church, is procreation. Secondary ends, such as mutual love, physical pleasure or the "quieting of concupiscence," can be satisfied only in their proper relationship to this primary end; that is, only when they are "subordinate" to it. Contraceptives, in the Catholic view, reverse this relationship by frustrating the primary end while permitting the satisfaction of secondary ends. They are therefore considered to be contrary to the law of nature and intrinsically evil.

Upon the priesthood of the church fell the task of justifying this doctrine before the bar of public opinion. Around 1915, just as the American birth control movement was getting under way, a counteractive stream of books, pamphlets and magazine articles began to pour from the Catholic clergy under the imprimaturs and *nihil obstats* of the church's censorship authorities.

Material for this article is drawn from the author's recent book, Birth Control and Catholic Doctrine, *Boston, Beacon Press, 1959.*

Catholic priests, doctors and laymen appeared before congressional and legislative committees to speak against proposed liberalization of federal and state laws prohibiting contraceptives.

To read the early literature against contraception is to enter into a phrase coiner's paradise. The difference between a woman who uses contraceptives and one who accepts the birth of children in accordance with nature's law is called the difference between a prostitute and a madonna. The Reverend Daniel A. Lord sums up this view: "Her body is no longer to be the sacred temple of life, but the object of man's desires and appetites."[1] The marriage bed becomes a "brothel"; intercourse becomes "mutual masturbation" and "reciprocal vice." By removing the fear of pregnancy, contraception leads to "marital infidelity, illicit love affairs, and ultimately polygamy."

From a medical standpoint, Catholic priests and doctors paint the consequences of contraception as dire: divine retribution for violating God's command to increase and multiply. Predictions of cancer, fibroids, sterility, neuroses and neurasthenia hang like an executioner's axe over the head of a woman who uses contraceptives, although there is no evidence whatsoever that methods of contraception approved and recommended by reputable non-Catholic doctors and the Planned Parenthood Federation will have any such effects.

Most of these ailments allegedly caused by contraceptives are attributed to the elimination or postponement of childbearing. In this category are "Malthusian uterus" and "chronic stasis," a supposed effect of "engorgment resulting from coitus and not interrupted by normal pregnancies." We are also cautioned that "emotional toxins" stimulated by "avoidance of parenthood" will lead to "functional disorders." Typical of this view is the classic statement of Sir Robert Armstrong Jones, M.D., F.R.C.P.S., quoted by Edward Roberts Moore in his *The Case Against Birth Control:* "[Birth control] leads to lunacy in women. If you are going to have birth control on a large scale you will have to add lunatic asylums for the mothers. The absence of children leads

---

(1) Daniel A. Lord, *Speaking of Birth Control*, St. Louis, The Queen's Work, Inc., 1930, p. 7.

to neurasthenia in married women, and that leads to insanity. I know from my own practice that that is a fact."[2]

The converse of the argument that contraceptives are medically harmful is the argument that large families are good for both the mother and the children. Pre-Rhythm Catholic writers on birth control see no reason why the ordinary woman should not bear from six to ten children with beneficial results. Case histories indicating physical and economic hardship resulting from large families are characterized as exceptions, and the writers tend to minimize such cases as that of a woman with a heart or kidney ailment for whom another pregnancy might be fatal. Catholic spokesmen conclude that a woman who is too sick to get pregnant is too sick to have intercourse.

As for the children, those living in large families are said to be less exposed to character damage from overly materialistic surroundings than children in small families. Calculated child-spacing is belittled, either on the ground that children of the same general age educate each other in the nursery, or on the ground that if modern women would only nurse their children through the "normal" lactation period, nature would space the birth of future children automatically.

In describing the economic implications of contraception, these early Catholic spokesmen present a lugubrious picture. Smaller families, they tell us, are a sure-fire guarantee of financial disaster, since they reduce the number of people who buy and sell, produce and consume. As the Reverend John A. Ryan observed before a subcommittee of the Senate Judiciary Committee in May 1932:

The demand for the products of the farms has considerably diminished. A few of the largest cities will continue to increase in population for some time yet, but by accretion from without instead of natural growth from within. The vast majority of our cities and towns can not expect any further growth. Hence the future looks very dark for the real estate business and the building trades. Indeed, the outlook is discouraging for all our indus-

---

(2) Quoted in Edward R. Moore, *The Case Against Birth Control*, New York, 1931, p. 28.

tries, inasmuch as our entire economic life heretofore has been based upon a continually increasing population.

At another hearing, in January 1934, he shed more tears for the real estate and construction businesses:

> I would hate to be in the real estate business in any city from now on. Of course, there will be income from commissions, but there will be no more big real-estate developments, because the people will not be there.
> What is going to happen to the construction industry?
> The steel industry, I venture, will never again in our lifetime reach the point it reached in 1929.

Further, Catholics charge, birth control perpetrates a fraud upon the working classes by depriving them of the joys of parenthood while evading the issues of the "economic wage" and "improved working conditions."

It is with respect to the social implications of birth control, however, that Catholic writers have managed to produce their most challenging forecasts. Birth control leads to "race suicide"; indeed, a nation which permits its population to decline *deserves* extinction. Early Catholic literature and the statements of Catholic witnesses at legislative committee hearings are filled with long statistical discussions of the population problem, all predicting either the disappearance of the race as a whole or its ultimate subjugation by the peoples of the Orient. The danger of overpopulation, one of the most imminent threats to human survival, is dismissed as a "phantom."

As an alternative to the use of contraceptives, Catholic writers before 1932 preached the virtues of absolute continence. Arduous and difficult though continence may be, it is said to "enrich the love life, reinforce the mutual affections, enhance mutual respect, and invest the home with new sanctities."[3] Comparison is made to the supposed continence of warriors and athletes, and it is portrayed as representing the triumph of the spirit over the desires of the flesh. In teaching that continence

---

(3) Charles P. Bruehl, *Birth Control and Eugenics*, New York, 1928, p. 36.

is the only method of birth control open to Catholics, Reverend Charles P. Bruehl explains, the church is teaching that "suffering is infinitely better than degradation and brutalization, and that spiritual freedom in pain is more desirable than voluptuous enslavement."[4] While the virtues of continence are admittedly somewhat dubious, the church has no choice but to recommend this alternative to its parishioners.

In 1932, as one Catholic clergyman proclaimed, Divine Providence came to the assistance of the church with a new medical discovery that showed a way out of this dilemma "without a compromise of principle." According to Doctors K. Ogino and H. Knaus, originators of the new method, it is unnecessary to avoid intercourse throughout the entire female menstrual cycle as an alternative to contraception. Their research disclosed that conception is possible only during about eight days of each month (including a margin of safety to compensate for difficulties of computation). A couple may therefore have normal sexual relations for all except this eight day period without the risk of conceiving a child. The Ogino-Knaus theory — or the Rhythm, as it is often called — presupposes an ability to predict the date of ovulation in the female menstrual cycle, either by keeping systematic records over a period of many months, a method which is vulnerable to future irregularities in the cycle, or by recording with a thermometer observable changes in body temperature, a method which is probably more accurate but by no means foolproof.

A somewhat cryptic passage in Pius XI's 1930 encyclical *Casti Connubii* paved the way for a subsequent express approval of the Rhythm by Pius XII. "Nor are those considered as acting against nature," Pius XI had written, "who in the married state use their right in the proper manner, although on account of natural reasons either of time or certain defects, new life cannot be brought forth." Catholic writers after 1932 interpreted the phrase "natural reasons . . . of time" as a reference to the menopause — or perhaps even to the so-called Capellman theory,

---

(4) *Ibid.*, p. 37.

a nineteenth century version of the Rhythm, memorable chiefly because it did not work. Moreover, the church had never forbidden intercourse in cases of permanent sterility, so that limiting marital relations to a "natural" but temporary sterile period was consistent with this established rule.

Not so easy to reconcile was the problem of how a married couple could confine intercourse to the infertile period, thus pursuing exclusively the secondary ends, when (as Pius XI said) such ends must be "subordinate to the primary end of procreation." When intercourse is so confined, is not pleasure a primary concern? The heretical implications of such an opinion were so great that the Holy See condemned it by decree in 1944. Nevertheless, in his 1951 Address to the Catholic Midwives, Pius XII confirmed the interpretation of his predecessor's encyclical as permitting the use of the safe period; he expressly approved the Rhythm as an acceptable alternative to both contraception and absolute continence. At the same time, he recognized the basic problem inherent in the church's new position, saying that continuous intercourse by married couples during the infertile period "without serious reason" would be a "sin against the very meaning of conjugal life."

Immediately after 1932, the safe-period method of birth control acted as the springboard for a new kind of Catholic literature. Whereas the earlier publications had explained why the church condemns contraception, Catholic priests and doctors now began writing practical handbooks on how to limit the size of the family by the use of the Rhythm. These books were unique in that they contained explicit birth control instructions. While some of the learned ecclesiastical journals anxiously debated whether knowledge of the Rhythm should be publicized indiscriminately or divulged only by the priesthood to penitents in confession, these handbooks bearing the imprimaturs and "ecclesiastical approbations" of Catholic bishops became best sellers. Dr. Leo J. Latz's *The Rhythm of Sterility and Fertility in Women,* for example, has gone through twenty-five printings and sold more than five hundred thousand copies.

Religion and science joined forces in this post-Rhythm literature to transform the earlier Catholic viewpoint on three phases of the subject. First, the new literature extols the secondary ends of intercourse, elevating them to a loftier position in the matrimonial scale of values, an emphasis which undoubtedly provoked the condemnatory decree of the Holy See in 1944. "Sex," says Dr. Latz, "when used as intended by the Creator, preserves, deepens and intensifies married love; it is love's expression and fulfillment; it confirms and strengthens the marital bond."[5] Intercourse during the safe period, says another handbook, has its "utility in married life, since it serves to foster mutual love and to allay concupiscence and because the pleasure which accompanies the intercourse will incite the couple to make frequent use of it."[6]

Second, in the new literature, the old strictures about the virtues of absolute continence are severely qualified. No longer having to sell absolute continence as the only alternative to contraceptives, Catholic post-Rhythm writers concede that it imposes an unbearable strain on married life. It involves "a tremendous and exalted sacrifice,"[7] and "may have a profound psychological effect on the man and on the woman, and may jeopardize the happiness of the marriage."[8] "Abstinence as a form of family limitation, particularly in young married people, is not only a difficult undertaking, but the repercussions from it might outweigh the advantages and reasons for its adoption."[9]

Third, medical science, to which no praise was given for the development of contraceptives, is hailed in the post-Rhythm literature as the handmaid of religion:

(5) Leo J. Latz, *The Rhythm of Sterility and Fertility in Women*, Chicago, 6th rev. ed., 1940, pp. 127-28.

(6) Valere J. Coucke, and James J. Walsh, *The Sterile Period in Family Life*, New York, 1933, p. 7.

(7) Daniel A. Lord, *What of Lawful Birth Control*, St. Louis, The Queen's Work, Inc., 1935, p. 8.

(8) Halliday Sutherland, *Catholic Medical Guardian*, April 1932, p. 81. This passage is cited in many other sources.

(9) John Ryan and Alan Keenan, *Marriage, A Medical and Sacramental Study*, London, 1956, p. 117.

The fact is that the Church embraces with eagerness every new discovery of science. In her vast temple of truth every new secret teased from any of the varied segments of nature finds a prompt and hearty welcome. For the Church knows that every newly-discovered truth will not only harmonize with her deposit of religious truths, but will give additional reenforcement to them.[10]

Confidence is expressed in the judgment of the individual men and women who will decide under what circumstances to use the Rhythm.

Despite this expression of confidence in the judgment of the individual, the church has refused to give carte blanche to the use of Rhythm under all circumstances. Instead, Catholic post-Rhythm authors have laid down the requirement of the "just cause" or, as Pius XII said, "serious reason." A just cause can be any good medical, eugenic, economic or social reason; the purpose of the restriction is to rule out indiscriminate use of the Rhythm for selfish or materialistic purposes.

It is precisely in this area of the just cause that Catholic writers after 1932 found themselves snared in the logical trap they had unwittingly set for themselves in the pre-Rhythm literature. The Rhythm, whether used for just cause or not, limits the size of the family by separating intercourse from parenthood. In this respect, it is exactly like a contraceptive. Why, then, if the dire consequences formerly attributed to contraception have any reality, should not the same consequences result from the use of the Rhythm?

Some writers are aware of this problem, which has been graphically expressed by an unhappy husband whose wife used the Rhythm, and who wrote in a letter to *Liguorian:*

This is a terrific occasion of sin for me. I fight it with daily Mass, daily Communion, daily rosary. But the fight goes on and sometimes I fall. . . . But why should I have to fight this constant battle against temptation when one of the purposes of

(10) John A. O'Brien, *Legitimate Birth Control,* Huntington, Ind., Our Sunday Visitor Press, 1934, p. 54.

marriage is to help a man stay out of sin? . . . rhythm is not a cure all; it is dancing dynamite. . . .[11]

One authority foresees a "lamentable lowering of the moral level of the conjugal relation" if the Rhythm "is adopted from the very outset of married life."[12] Another observes that "the unwarranted practice of periodic continence often tends to make a slave of the woman, while awakening the beast in the man."[13]

To disengage themselves from this logical difficulty, the post-Rhythm authors hang on grimly to the concept of the just cause. Obviously, intercourse confined exclusively to the safe period is pragmatically indistinguishable from what the pre-Rhythm writers scored as "reciprocal vice." By removing the fear of pregnancy, the Rhythm can, like contraception, encourage illicit relations before marriage or in adultery. To the extent that it prevents conception, the same dire medical consequences should follow; the same economic disaster from fewer consumers should be inevitable; and race suicide should be our expected destiny. But somehow, Catholic spokesmen would have us believe, the just cause makes a difference. On the other hand, if the just cause *does* make it moral to limit families by use of the Rhythm, and if these supposedly inevitable dire consequences will *not* then occur, why will the just cause not have the same beneficial effect on contraception?

The point of this analysis is not to ridicule the plight of Catholic reason but to suggest the urgent need for a re-examination of the Catholic position. Before 1932, Catholic doctrine on birth control could be accepted as a logically worded statement of ecclesiastical dogma, even though one might disagree with it or deplore it. Now, however, with the church's approval of the Rhythm, the Catholic position no longer makes sense even within the framework of the church's own statements about it. To con-

---

(11) *Liguorian,* January 1957, p. 43.
(12) Raoul de Guchteneere, "Physical and Moral Consequences of the Knaus-Ogino Discovery," *Homiletic and Pastoral Review,* December 1933, p. 257.
(13) Orville N. Griese, *The Morality of Periodic Continence,* Washington, The Catholic University of America Press, 1942, pp. 63-64.

tinue to maintain this position in the face of human and international problems — particularly problems of overpopulation, which would benefit from the widespread use of contraceptives — does less than justice to the sound judgment and common sense of the Catholic hierarchy. At the moment, unfortunately, the church is so wedded to its doctrine on birth control that it refuses to take a realistic view of overpopulation problems, urging emigration and a better distribution of world resources but not family limitation as approved relief measures.

The way out of this dilemma is both simple and rational; it involves no change in the basic doctrine that procreation is the primary end of intercourse. The church need only declare that motives and circumstances, which it accepts as a test of the morality of the Rhythm, are an equally good index of the morality of contraception. It would thus extricate itself from a logical cul-de-sac, and would be in a position to exercise moral leadership in meeting the threatening problems of overpopulation in the many underdeveloped countries of the world.

A Sociologist Looks at Liberal Religion

by *Alfred McClung Lee*

As long ago as the eighteenth century, Unitarian writings were said "to unsettle everything, yet settle nothing." (The quotation is from a comment by Samuel Johnson on the theological works of the great scientist and Unitarian minister, Joseph Priestley.) Much the same appraisal has often been made of scientific sociology. In both cases, those who are unsettled are the orthodox, especially those fearful of intellectual adventure and of social change.

A sociologist examining liberal religion is quickly impressed by the calm with which Ethical Culturists, Friends, Humanists, Unitarians and Universalists view the implications of current social scientific research. Religious liberals apparently regard the scientific process as the only tenable process of what might be called revelation. Whether one wishes to call such revelation divine or not is an individual matter. As I understand it, one may call it human or divine, and still be a religious liberal. I am both a sociologist and a Unitarian, and I find nothing at all incompatible between the two.

I should like here to outline my impressions of what liberal religion should stress at this point in its history. In doing so, I shall not labor too much the interrelationships of science, democracy and liberal religion. Let us just assume that they are interrelated in an inextricable manner (so far as we here are concerned) and go on from there.

Liberal religion sensibly begins with faith in man. No one has been able to verify that he has seen or otherwise sensed a manlike God. You may or may not wish to go beyond faith in

This article is revised and adapted from articles published in The Christian Register, *February 1949, pp. 15-17, and* The Ethica' Outlook, *November-December 1956, pp. 186-190.*

man: that depends upon your own emotional and intellectual needs. In either case, you will not attempt, within a liberal meeting, to give your belief the force of a dogmatic mandate. In a liberal congregation there are no *Thou shalts* and *Thou shalt nots*. There is only the human conscience (or superego, or whatever you might wish to call it) — the social product of traditional human striving and individual aspirations.

You can go a long way toward developing a satisfying philosophy of life by trusting chiefly, or even exclusively, in the general decency of man and in the power of human beings inspired by ideals. To suggest how far a faith in man can take us, let me outline ten principles which I think we as Unitarians might well stress at this point in our history and in the history of mankind:

1. Faith in man.
2. Rejection of façades, and concern for realities.
3. Rejection of authoritarianism, but not of democratically vested and controlled authority.
4. Faith in democracy in the home.
5. Acceptance or rejection of people on their personal merits.
6. Encouragement of democracy in education.
7. Striving for democracy in government.
8. Support for organizations seeking to democratize business.
9. Promotion of scientific and democratic principles in philosophy and religion.
10. Rejection of enervating fatalism, and faith in a hope based on knowledge rather than on poetic speculation.

There is more than a slight parallel between a number of these principles and that ancient and admirable body of rules for belief and practice, the Ten Commandments. I have attempted to translate the Ten Commandments into democratic terms more closely related to modern, day-to-day living — to translate them, if you will, into a Unitarian decalogue.

As a motivation for people to adhere to these principles, we have, not the thunderous voice of a tribal deity, but the compulsion of enlightened human experience, evinced in a growing democratic spirit. As an object of faith, we have a hopeful image of man, rather than an idealized projection of man or his human authority figures into the supernatural realm. The term "graven images" is translated here as "façades." "Authoritarianism" is the "other gods" before which a religious liberal does not bow down. Relations among husband and wife, parents and children, are summarized as "faith in democracy in the home." Finally, because our society has become so complex, the nurturing of broader and sounder concepts of human relations in the various social fields is given more attention than in the God- and property-centered Ten Commandments.

Let us consider briefly each of the items in this Unitarian decalogue:

1. *Faith in man.* I do not think that all human beings are sweet and lovely. We start out as little animals unable to control our bodily functions; even after years of effort, frustration and cussedness, we never reach the ideals we and society set for ourselves. As a sociologist, I have spent my life studying social problems, including riots, strikes, wars, divorce, prostitution, exploitation, and juvenile and adult delinquency and crime. I am well aware that man's inhumanity to men is a pervasive and frightening reality. But if one analyzes a social problem thoroughly one sees how often it is caused by outworn social institutions, outworn allocations of social power and outworn human customs. Outworn social institutions coerce us into antisocial beliefs and practices. Given a chance to develop his latent creative and altruistic impulses, man can achieve tremendous feats in the arts, the sciences and the kindnesses which have made the finer aspects of our society.

2. *Rejection of façades, and concern for realities.* We must see through the glittering façades that traditionally surround our most revered institutions and institutional functionaries. We must determine whether the actual, operational realities of

those institutions and functionaries are true to their outward appearances. Or do the façades serve merely to hide from public view a disastrous corruption?

We have had endless and very disturbing instances of secret corruption in recent years. The political organizations of certain states and cities, for example, are in the hands of race-track syndicates. This is a pathological condition from which the antiseptic of virtuous intentions cannot protect us. We have had widespread reports of deception in education and the arts, from cheating on examinations to "payola" and the television quiz scandals. Let us be especially wary of the care and sophistication with which many established clergymen of major denominations excuse and rationalize the hypocrisy, the "materialism" and the "moral decay" of their own flocks, to whom they preach each Sunday morning.

3. *Rejection of authoritarianism, but not of democratically vested and controlled authority.* Authoritarian modes of thought persist and have a disturbing influence on us all. Even though the facts of social history, sociology and anthropology assign a modest role to the great man in any field, we still talk as though a whole liberal education can be gained by reading one hundred supposedly great books, or as though the whole course of history can be modified by a Hoover, a Roosevelt, a Truman or an Eisenhower.

When a man is democratically elected to an office of responsibility, and is made subject in his formulations of policy to popular pressures, we have established the least treacherous type of authority. We, the people, set up such a man and give him his authority, and we can easily replace him with another trustee of our authority. The people are often confused, and they make many mistakes; but they are far less confused as to their own best interests and far less mistaken in the long run than is any self-perpetuating individual or clique.

4. *Faith in democracy in the home.* The patterns of tension which threaten the welfare of our society and of the world begin in the home. Psychiatrists point out that overanxious mothers pass their anxieties on to their children from infancy. Distracted

middle-class fathers seldom spend enough time with their children to become well acquainted with them and to guide their maturation. Undemocratic homes produce frustrated, spoiled and brutalized children who spend the rest of their lives fighting out the patterns of their old family struggles. They do needless battle with their business, political, social and family associates. The solution is not that kind of so-called family democracy in which spoiled children oppress their parents, but a maturely conceived family democracy in which both parents and children come to know each other as human beings with mutual respect and understanding.

Basic to such family democracy is a sane and informed attitude toward sex and reproduction. For the health of the mother and her children — physically, emotionally, mentally and socially — births need to be spaced, and limited to the number the family can afford. Sane birth control in each family can help halt the vast population explosion so disastrously under way throughout the world.

5. *Acceptance or rejection of people on their personal merits.* People who inhabit the "nicer" residential districts frequently speak with disdain of those who involve themselves in race riots, the defacing of synagogues, the closing of public schools and other violent antiminority excesses. Social scientists, however, recognize two kinds of antiminority sentiment: the crude and the polite. Those who live in the "nicer" suburbs are guilty of polite antiminority sentiments and practices which are highly destructive influences on intergroup relations in this country and throughout the world.

It is the polite people who support the Greek-letter fraternities and sororities which nurture ethnic and racial snobbishness among our college students. It is the polite people who say that it is kinder not to invite a minority member into their women's clubs, men's service clubs, and business and professional clubs. Now that race-restrictive covenants on real estate have been declared unconstitutional by the United States Supreme Court, and a start has been made toward school integration, the pillars of many of our "nice" churches in our "better" residential dis-

tricts, especially in the North, are finding polite ways to evade
the law.

Polite — or even unconscious — discrimination is contrary
to liberal religion as I understand it. We must grasp the hands
of our fellows around the world, of every race, color, religion and
ethnic stock. We must find ways and means to understand them
and to live in peace with them.

6. *Encouragement of democracy in education.* In many public schools and colleges today, there are overwhelming pressures
to de-emphasize the student as an object of the teacher's concern
and to pervert free and honest standards of teaching and research.
The emphasis has swung away from the development of enlightened minds, minds adaptable to the varied conditions and
challenges of human life. It has swung toward the fashioning
of "well-rounded" technicians who will mesh with other "well-
rounded" technicians in our business and governmental bu-
reaucracies. More and more, our students bypass the arts,
humanities and sciences with which all enlightened citizens of
the twentieth century should be acquainted.

A faith in democracy in education implies a faith that the
human mind has potentialities for good when it is free to grow
in a stimulating and broadening environment. The arbitrary
dismissal of popular but irritating teachers — or the refusal to
hire them — is destructive of such an environment. The reduc-
tion of a high school and college education to a mere acquisition
of the tools of a trade inevitably cripples our future citizens.

7-8. *Striving for democracy in government and Support for
organizations seeking to democratize business.* These two principles are closely related in our society because government
and business have become more and more intricately interrelated,
especially during this century. The day of cynical bosses who
buy cheap votes from their followers and sell them to big business is passing. Their followers have learned that their votes can
be used directly to insure their own social welfare. The day of
cynical Taft-Hartley acts and of "steel deals" for the glory of
political candidates will also pass. Both management and labor
must face their new responsibilities and privileges as an increas-

ingly higher degree of industrial democracy is achieved.

International peace is our most pressing problem, yet here our discussion seems most paralyzed. All religious liberals can learn a great lesson from the Friends, who have always sensed a power in the testimony of *even one* concerned individual, such as the conscientious objector to the war system. The power of one such courageous dissenter is far greater than even he often suspects.

9. *Promotion of scientific and democratic principles in philosophy and religion.* Down through the ages, churches have frequently been citadels of intellectual and even political and economic authoritarianism. When a priest engaged in special pleading, he certified it with a formula such as "Thus spake the Lord God Almighty." His flock could scarcely question such an authority. Only with the rise of antiauthoritarian religions and philosophies, such as those grouped around Unitarianism, have congregations ceased to be subjected to these pretensions. When a speaker states his position in a liberal religious meeting, his ideas receive scrutiny and discussion before they are regarded as any more than one man's view.

When a man achieves sufficient dignity and self-respect to face the cosmos, the earth and his fellow men without the old, dogmatic guides to direct him, his potentialities for development are vastly increased. Instead of "moral chaos" and "materialism" and "a lack of spiritual values," he will experience a surging forward of the human spirit, motivated by a morality and by spiritual values which are impervious to changing social conditions — because they are in tune with conditions as they change.

10. *Rejection of enervating fatalism, and faith in a hope based on knowledge rather than on poetic speculation.* When one first learns that there is no Santa Claus, or that babies are not brought by a stork, or that sex and aggression play tremendous roles in our lives, one may feel a sense of loss. Life is not so glamorous, just after an illusion of childhood has been destroyed. But to those who can face knowledge without hysteria and who want to learn from verified observations of natural

phenomena, the wonders of birth remain wonders even when they are realistically understood. The marvels and perplexities of psychology and sociology become all the more absorbing when one studies realities rather than folklore.

Even though such an early disillusionment may pass and be replaced by an enthusiastic curiosity, there is another type of enervating fatalism which arises from a little knowledge of science. It is the fatalism of the person who says, especially in the social realm, that a given problem involves so many and such weighty factors that an individual can do little to correct it. Prostitution, for example, persists because influential people control the institutions which own the property in which brothels operate, protected by a police force which is often answerable to private influence. So what can we do? Alcoholism cannot be eliminated by prohibition; so what can we do? Some persons even contend that laws and court decisions *retard* the integration of racial and religious minorities. Such attitudes are the off-springs of inadequate knowledge of the situations in question.

There are few human social problems which, when carefully and adequately studied, cannot be at least mitigated by well-designed reform programs. A Communist hates and fears most the reformers and libertarians who effectively counteract such social ills. An immediate and complete victory is seldom gained in a struggle against such social problems as gangster-ridden race tracks, racial segregation, prostitution, alcoholism and low educational standards. But with careful planning and determined efforts, great strides can be made.

The poetic, artistic imagination is, of course, important. It makes life beautiful and endurable, and it reveals ideas that might or might not be true. The danger comes when we confuse the truth of beauty with its objective verification. Beauty need not be verifiable to be eternally entrancing and essential to man; but when we confuse this truth with the immediate social realities, we delude ourselves disastrously. This is a perennial weakness of many intellectuals in the West and possibly everywhere — but, luckily, not of all.

If one is satisfied to make what contributions one can to

human welfare, satisfied with the personal and social gains of fighting *for* human values rather than *against* them, the faith and practices of liberal religion offer both a philosophy and a program of life.